TRIADSOLOING**FOR**
MODERNGUITAR

Master Triad Shapes, Creative Patterns & Triad Pairs for Articulate, Melodic Guitar Soloing

OZ**NOY**

FUNDAMENTAL**CHANGES**

Triad Soloing For Modern Guitar

Master Triad Shapes, Creative Patterns & Triad Pairs for Articulate, Melodic Guitar Soloing

ISBN: 978-1-78933-474-6

Published by **www.fundamental-changes.com**

Copyright © 2025 Oz Noy

Edited by Tim Pettingale

www.fundamental-changes.com

Join our free Facebook Community of Cool Musicians

www.facebook.com/groups/fundamentalguitar

Instagram: **FundamentalChanges**

For over 350 Free Guitar Lessons with Videos Check Out

www.fundamental-changes.com

Cover Image Copyright: Author photo, used by permission.

Contents

Introduction.. 4

Get the Audio.. 7

Chapter One – Major Triads 8

Chapter Two – Minor Triads... 38

Chapter Three – Augmented Triads.. 63

Chapter Four – Diminished Triads.. 84

Conclusion & Practice Plan 108

Introduction

Triads! Guitar players know that they are the simplest, most fundamental of musical building blocks we have as musicians, but few ever gain real mastery over them. Why is this? While almost every player knows exactly how a major triad sounds, when asked to play that triad all over the fretboard, most are left scratching their heads and can only play a few shapes and positions. The truth is, triads are an area of technique that we *know* we should know, but never spend enough time on.

I hope to change that with this book, because understanding how to manipulate triads will open up a vast new world of melodic possibilities to you.

For the modern guitarist who wants to play jazz, rock, blues, fusion or other styles, a thorough knowledge of triads is essential. They are the foundation on which we build all the chords we play, and they form the core of our melodic vocabulary.

Triads are a powerful and practical tool for improvisation. We can use them to outline chord changes, create more colorful sounds by superimposing them over chords to create upper extensions, and use them to effectively navigate modal vamps. Triads offer the most direct way to create sophisticated sounds with a highly melodic approach. In the right hands, they stop being simple building blocks and become vehicles for groove, color and some highly modern sounds.

The good news is that you only need to focus on learning *four* triads, from which every other type of chord is constructed:

- Major

- Minor

- Augmented (which you can think of as a close relative of the major)

- Diminished (which you can think of as a close relative of the minor)

In this book, I'm going to give you an easy-to-follow method for learning each of these triads all over the fretboard, then show you how to incorporate triad-based ideas into your solos.

Step 1: Visualize the Triad Across the Neck

Initially playing the triad as chord voicings, you'll learn to play it all over the fretboard.

- First as *closed voice* chords (arranged on three adjacent strings)

- Second, as *open voiced* chords (arranged with a string skip)

Step 2: Learn Essential Triad Patterns

You'll learn a series of exercises that will serve two important purposes: first, they will strengthen your ability to visualize and play each triad across the neck. Second, the exercises themselves can develop into melodic phrases and can be used as patterns and sequences in your solos. The primary patterns are:

- Jumping 3rds

- Jumping 3rds alternative pattern

- String skipped 5ths or contrary motion

Step 3: Enclosure Patterns

Next, you'll work on enhancing triad patterns by playing them as enclosures. We'll start simply by adding single notes above or below the notes of the triad, and build towards more complex patterns. These are great exercises, but you should also think of them of cellular melodic ideas that will become a part of your improvisation vocabulary. Here's the method you'll follow:

- Play the triad all over the fretboard, adding a note a half step below each triad note to form a pattern

- Repeat the exercise, this time adding a note a half step above each triad note

- Add notes below and above to create a repeating cellular pattern

- Flip that pattern and play above, then below

- Next, play note combinations above and below each triad note, combining diatonic (scale) and chromatic notes to create another set of melodic patterns

- Finally, play chromatic enclosures that encircle each triad note to create five-note cells

Step 4: Triad Pairs Primer

Many modern players use *triad pairs* to create more sophisticated sounds when soloing. The essence of this idea is to select two triads from the parent key we're playing in, and combine them to create melodic ideas. For example, we might combine C major and E minor triads.

To create more edgy sounds we can "borrow" triads from other scales (called *modal interchange*) and put together triads that don't exist in the same key, such as C major and F# major (i.e., the major triad a flattened 5th above C).

When you become fluent at switching between them, triad pairs can really elevate your musical vocabulary. However, this is a big area of study that could fill several books all on its own! Here, my purpose is just to whet your appetite to explore this idea more deeply.

Step 5: Add9 Triad Sounds

Finally, an important idea in the vocabulary of modern players is the add9 sound. This is as simple as it sounds: we take a basic triad and add a 9th interval to create a four-note cell.

You'll have heard this sound used extensively by players such as Allan Holdsworth, Wayne Krantz, Mike Stern, Julian Lage, Eric Johnson and Jonathan Kreisberg. This is another big area of study which we can only dip into, but you can apply the principles you learn here and work on this concept on your own.

When you've worked through the exercises for a particular triad type, you'll then move on to learn a solo that showcases that triad. Working on the solo (either as a whole or in sections – just focusing on the licks you like) will help you to understand how to use these ideas in a real-world musical context.

You'll hear many of the patterns you've learned being used and (most importantly) blended with other musical ideas, such as pentatonic runs, bends and scale sequences. You have the backing tracks for these tunes in the free audio download, so make sure you jam over them and try out all the ideas in the book as well as creating your own.

Have fun with it!

Oz

Get the Audio

The audio files for this book are available to download for free from **www.fundamental-changes.com.** The link is in the top right-hand corner. Click on the "Guitar" link then simply select this book title from the drop-down menu and follow the instructions to get the audio.

We recommend that you download the files directly to your computer, not to your tablet, and extract them there before that adds them to your media library.

For over 350 free guitar lessons with videos check out:

www.fundamental-changes.com

Join our free Facebook Community of Cool Musicians

www.facebook.com/groups/fundamentalguitar

Tag us for a share on Instagram: **FundamentalChanges**

Chapter One – Major Triads

Every chord we play on guitar is built from the notes of a parent scale. In Western Harmony, we use a *tertian* system of intervals to create a chord. This means we build chords by stacking intervals in 3rds.

To construct a basic, three-note C major chord (known as a triad) we begin with the C Major scale (C, D, E, F, G, A, B). We take the first note (C), stack a 3rd interval on top (the note E), then stack another 3rd interval (G) on top of that.

The resulting notes (C, E, G) form a C major triad with a root note, a major 3rd and a perfect 5th.

The first step toward knowing your triads inside out is to be able to play them anywhere on the fretboard. There are a few systems for learning triad shapes, but the one I favor is to learn them horizontally across the neck, arranged on string sets.

As soon as we start playing triads in this way, one thing immediately becomes apparent:

On each string set there are just *three shapes* to learn that *repeat* across the neck.

Once you've grasped this concept, you'll find it much easier to remember the triad shapes, and it'll be easier for you to transpose them to other keys. Let's look at the shapes organized by string sets, from low to high.

Step 1: Visualize the Triad Across the Neck

First, here are the three major triad shapes arranged on strings 6, 5 & 4, beginning with the shape that has its root note on the sixth string.

First we play the triad in root position, then 1st inversion, then 2nd inversion. The shapes repeat in this order across the neck.

The diagram below is labelled by interval, showing the location of the root note for each shape. This will make it easier for you to transpose these shapes to any key.

Diagram 1

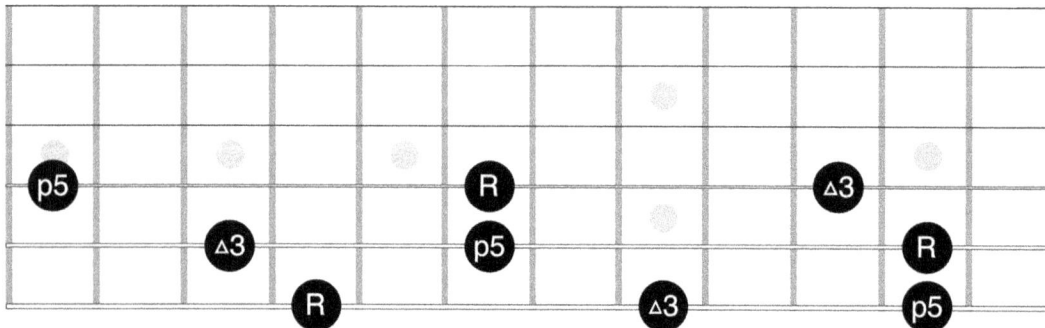

Next, the three major triad shapes on strings 5, 4 & 3, beginning with the fifth string root note shape, followed by 1st and 2nd inversion shapes.

Diagram 2

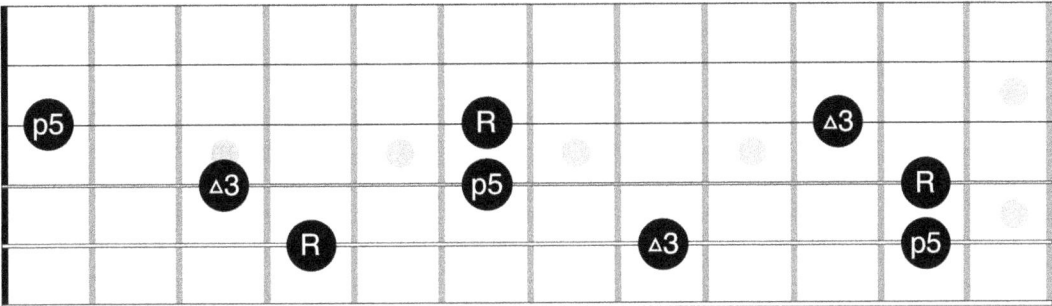

Now we have the three major triad shapes arranged on strings 4, 3 & 2.

Diagram 3

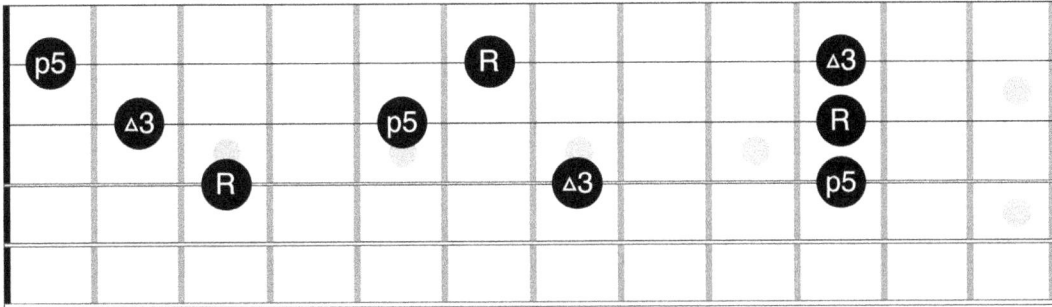

And lastly, the three major triad shapes on strings 3, 2 & 1.

Diagram 4

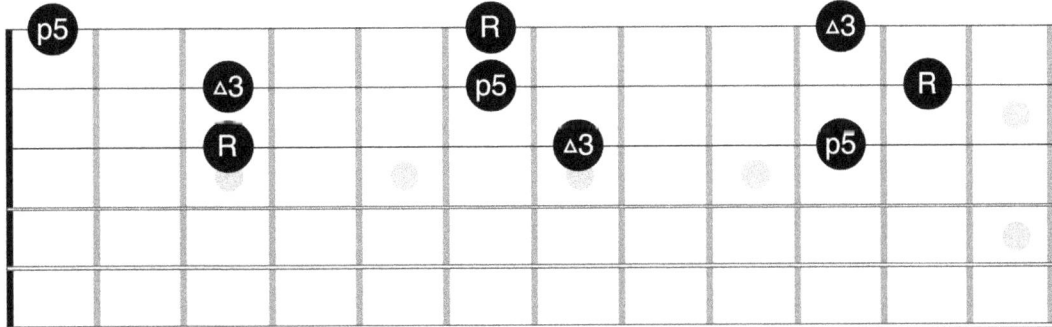

These diagrams have shown you *all* the locations on the fretboard where you can play *closed voiced* major triads. "Closed voiced" means that the notes are arranged on three adjacent strings. (Shortly, we'll look at how we can play them as "open voiced" triads, which introduces a string skip).

It's important to learn these shapes thoroughly so that you can play them anywhere on the neck. Then, when you want to solo using triads, you'll be able to move easily between them. In a moment we'll walk through some important drills to do that, but first, we'll practice how to play C major triad chords horizontally across the neck on each string set.

In Example 1a we start on the lowest string set and work our way onto the highest string set. This drill will help to reinforce the triad shapes and help you to memorize the relationship between the intervals.

Make it your goal to learn this exercise by memory, then test yourself. First, play to a metronome or drum groove and play the shapes in sequence across string sets. Then comp with the shapes and see if you can mix them up, moving freely between string sets. This will soon tell you how well you know them!

Don't shortcut spending time with these shapes, because they will provide you with a great musical foundation for what follows.

Example 1a – Closed Voiced Major Triads

We can also play C major triads across the neck as *open voiced* shapes. Where closed voiced triads sound dense and are contained within a single octave, open voiced triads sound more spacious and span more than one octave. It's useful to know these shapes for chord playing and comping. Open voiced triads play a large role in the rhythm style of guitarists like Eric Johnson and others.

An open voiced triad must include a string skip. The two most common approaches to playing them are:

- Two notes on adjacent strings, a string skip, then the third note

- One note, a string skip, then two notes on adjacent strings

You'll see both types in the next exercise. Here we mix and match voicings simply because they are easier to play and any avoid big fretting hand stretches.

(NB: I know that it's possible to play open voiced triads with multiple string skips, but these are much less practical to play so I tend to avoid them).

Example 1b – Open Voiced C Major Triads

Step 2: Essential Triad Patterns

The next step is to learn the major triad across the neck with some pattern-based exercises. These act like a bridge between simply knowing the triad as a series of three-note clusters across the fretboard and turning them into real music.

I call this first drill the jumping 3rds pattern. Refer back to the three major triad shapes shown in Diagram 1 and you'll see that this melodic sequence launches from each of them in turn.

The idea here is that alternate notes of the triad are played in a continuous sequence (e.g., C, G, E, C, etc.) – never in a root–3rd–5th configuration.

Play through this exercise very slowly and memorize the sequence of intervals in each triad position and how they sound. Aim to pick everything cleanly, efficiently, and with a good tone before you even think of speeding up! It's important to train your muscle memory really well.

Your end goal is to be able to play this smoothly and cleanly at 120bpm and beyond, but don't run until you can walk.

Example 1c

Here is an alternative way to play jumping 3rds, beginning from the 5th string root position and using a pattern that crawls across the neck, rather than remaining in position.

Example 1d

This next drill, which I call jumping 5ths for short, uses a contrary motion idea to move across the fretboard.

The *lowest* of each pair of notes ascends a C major triad from the root, then descends it (bars 1-3). The *top* note of each pair ascends then descends the triad in 2nd inversion.

At the end of bar three, from beat 4 onwards, the lowest note of each pair ascends the triad in 1st inversion, while the top note ascends/descends the triad from the root.

This is better heard than read, so have a careful listen to the audio.

This is a more challenging exercise to play with all the string skips and position changes, so work through it slowly, figuring out the most comfortable fingering, and memorize the intervals and the sound they make.

Example 1e

Lastly, here's an exercise which doesn't follow an intervallic pattern. We are just ascending and descending the C major triad all over the neck, moving freely between positions. This is a good way to test if you've really grasped the layout of the triad across the fretboard. You can invent your own versions of this exercise.

Example 1f

Step 3: Enclosure Patterns

Over many years of teaching students, I've found that a great way to reinforce any triad or arpeggio shape is to apply enclosure patterns to it. In other words, to add chromatic approach notes below or above the triad notes in various combinations.

We're going to explore this idea thoroughly, as these patterns can form the basis of musical phrases and sequences you can incorporate into your solos.

In Example 1g play the C major triad across the neck, placing an approach note a half step *below* each triad note.

Example 1g

Now reverse that pattern and place an approach note *above* each note of the C major triad. This creates quite a tense, exotic sound, but the point of the exercise is to test how well you know the locations of the triad notes.

Example 1h

Next, we'll drill the triad with approach notes placed *below* then *above* the triad notes, before we play the triad note itself.

Example 1i

Now we'll flip that pattern and place approach notes *above* then *below* the triad notes.

Example 1j

Things become more musical when we enclose the triad notes with an approach note a half step below, and a note from the C Major parent scale above.

Example 1k

The next drill is a chromatic enclosure exercise. This enclosure pattern is a common bebop device that creates a five-note cell. The idea is to play a note a half step below the target triad tone, then two notes above that descend chromatically to the triad tone, then the same note a half step below, before finally playing the triad tone.

As a result, this is quite a long exercise, but the addition of the approach notes helps us to focus on where the triad tones are located. It's also a great alternate picking drill!

Example 1l

Measures 9–11 (TAB):
```
                                                          12-15-14-12-13
                                          11-14-13-11-12
            9-12-11-9-10    9-12-11-9-10   13-16-15-13-14
11-14-13-11-12
```

Measures 12–14 (TAB):
```
11-14-13-11-12   14-17-16-14-15   11-14-13-11-12
                                  12-15-14-12-13
                                                  11-14-13-11-12
                                                  13-16-15-13-14
```

Measures 15–17 (TAB):
```
   9-12-11-9-10
             9-12-11-9-10                            14-17-16-14-15
                          11-14-13-11-12   14-17-16-14-15
```

Measures 18–20 (TAB):
```
                                          14-17-16-14-15   19-22-21-19-20
              11-14-13-11-12   12-15-14-12-13   16-19-18-16-17
13-16-15-13-14
```

Measures 21–24 (TAB):
```
14-17-16-14-15
            16-19-18-16-17   12-15-14-12-13
                                   11-14-13-11-12
                                          13-16-15-13-14
                                              14-17-16 14-15
                                                        14-17-16 14-15
```

In the previous exercise we played the enclosures as distinct five-note cells, but this idea lends itself to constructing sequenced licks like the one below, played using continuous 1/16th notes. The result is a cascading, descending pattern. After hearing the enclosures as separate cells, it can take a minute to get used to the sound of them shifting across the beat, but this is a much more interesting idea. On your own, figure out how to reverse this sequence and play it from low to high.

Example 1m

Step 4: Triad Pairs Primer

In this next section, we're going to dip into a concept known as *triad pairs*. I call this a primer, because the topic could warrant a whole book of its own. I wanted to briefly explain the idea here, however, because it's a feature of my playing style and an idea you can work on in your practice sessions.

Soloing with triad pairs is a powerful tool for improvisation – one that can immediately open the door to new harmonic and melodic possibilities. The idea is to pair two triads and alternate between them. The triads are often taken from the same parent scale, but we can also "borrow" non-diatonic triads from different scales, depending on whether we want to create inside or more outside sounds.

For example, if we're playing over a C major chord, we could pair C major and D minor triads (diatonic triads from the parent key of C Major).

The C major triad simply spells out the chord tones, but the D minor triad, when superimposed over a C major chord, creates some extended intervals.

Dm contains the notes D, F, A. Over a C major chord they represent the 9th, 11th and 13th intervals.

So you can think of using triad pairs as a quick, easy route to creating more colorful melodic lines.

However, we can also "borrow" non-diatonic triads, or triads based on an interval. An idea I like to use, demonstrated in the next few examples, is to take a major triad and pair it with another major triad a flattened 5th above. E.g., a C major triad paired with an F# major triad.

This sound has been used by many jazz musicians (you may have heard George Benson playing licks based on this idea) and it instantly creates an *inside-outside-inside* repeating pattern. Let's look at a few ways to play it.

First, have a listen to the sound that the triad pair makes. Because we are alternating them in this example, you can clearly hear how the movement starts inside the harmony, goes outside, then moves back inside etc.

This idea gives us the stable C major triad, plus the tension notes introduced by the F# major triad. The notes of the latter (F#, A#, C#) create #11, b7 and b9 intervals over the C major chord, briefly implying a C altered dominant harmony.

Example 1n

To really get inside this idea, we can apply the drill patterns we used earlier. Here are C major and F# major triads, played in the jumping 3rds pattern.

As soon as we apply this pattern, it creates a much more complex melodic line and it's harder to hear the triads alternating. However, we can still hear the inside-outside movement.

Example 1o

Here is the alternate jumping 3rds pattern we learned earlier containing more string skips, now applied to C major and F# major triad pairs.

Example 1p

You'll see practically how this idea can be put into use when you work through the solo study at the end of this chapter.

Step 5: Add9 Triad Sounds

Another important sound in triad soloing is the add9 triad form. This is a major triad with an added 9th (the second degree of the parent scale, moved into the higher octave) – not to be confused with a major 9 chord.

We spell a Cadd9 chord: C, D, E, G

When played as chords, add9s make a bright, spacious sound, and are less dense sounding than major 9 chords. The way add9 voicings fall on the fretboard means that it's easy to place the 9th on top, which adds to their spacey, chiming sound.

When soloing, the add9 triad gives us a useful four-note melodic cell that sounds very stable, but adds some harmonic sophistication. It also helps us to break away from playing dense scalic runs all the time. You'll hear add9 sounds in the improvisation of players like Eric Johnson, Wayne Krantz, Tim Miller, Jonathan Kreisberg and Matteo Mancuso.

Here is the Cadd9 arpeggio pattern played ascending and descending.

Example 1q

Next, let's apply the jumping 3rds pattern we used earlier.

Example 1r

Starting and ending in the root position, here is a different path we can take to spell out the Cadd9 triad.

Example 1s

To make things rhythmically more interesting, let's play the jumping 3rds pattern again, this time played with an 1/8th note triplet rhythm. This is a little more challenging because sometimes we have to cross strings mid-triplet, and sometimes we have to play several triplets on one string to keep the pattern going.

Example 1t

Another common idea to sequence an add9 triad is to ascend or descend in "4s". Here, we ascend four notes from the root of the triad, then go back to the second note in the sequence and ascend four notes from there, and so on. Once you hear this idea, you'll immediately get it.

In the early bars, it's easy to hear the pattern, but to make the drill more difficult, we descend immediately without replaying the E note on the first string, 12th fret – which means that on the way down, the four-note cells fall on different beats of the bar. It's harder to hear the pattern this way, but it's good for making us focus on visualizing the pattern and listen out for the note intervals.

Example 1u

There is a lot of work in these drills and you should keep practicing them as much as you can. When you're very comfortable with a particular pattern, move it to other keys. Or, for a serious challenge, work out how to play it through the Circle of Fifths.

Solo Study

Now we're going to break down a solo I played that showcases major triads over the changes to the jazz standard *St Thomas* by Sonny Rollins. The full solo is notated at the end of this chapter, but I want to highlight certain bars to show where I used the ideas we've been looking at.

Chord Tone Targeting

Before we look at specific ideas, let me say that my overall approach with this tune was one of chord tone targeting. *St Thomas* has fast moving chord changes and to play melodically it's useful to spell out those changes. The first eight bars of the solo are a good example of this approach.

A simple explanation of chord tone targeting is that we aim to play chord tones on downbeats most of the time. This isn't a hard and fast rule, but having strong chord tones *mostly* falling on the beat helps to clearly spell out the harmony.

In bar one, we begin by highlighting the 5th and root of the C6 chord, then play a phrase that targets an F note at the beginning of bar two – the 3rd of Dm7. This phrase ascends to target a B note, the 3rd of G7.

The 3rd is often the strongest chord tone to highlight apart from the root, but we can target other chord tones and extended or even altered tones. For example, in bar five we repeat a G note (the b3 of Em7b5), then target a C# note over the Bb7 chord. This note implies a harmony of Bb7#9. On beat 4 of this bar, we drop another C# note, this time over A7, which is the 3rd of that chord.

Take a look also at the beginning of bar seven, where we begin with an E note (3rd of C major), then play a descending phrase that places a Bb note on beat 2, which is the b7 of the C7 chord.

Example 1v

C   C9/E   F   F#dim   C6/G   G7   C6

(TAB notation)

Jumping 3rds Pattern

There are a few places in the solo where I briefly phrased passages in 3rds, but bar eleven is one of the clearest examples. Check out bars 10-12 of the full solo TAB to see how I got into and out of this idea.

Example 1w

C6   Em7   A7

(TAB notation)

Bar thirty-nine of the solo is another example of jumping 3rds (shown as bar two below). Notice that I begin the 3rds pattern at the end of the preceding bar, over the G7 chord. Here I'm playing jumping 3rds from a G major triad, then moving into a C major triad over the C6 chord. From there, I transition into an FMaj7 arpeggio for the second half of the bar.

Example 1x

Dm7   Ab7   G7   C6   C9/E   F   F#dim

(TAB notation)

Add9 Triads

Earlier we looked at expanding the basic major triad by adding the 9th interval. This gives us a four-note Cadd9 cell we can build melodic ideas from. The fast 1/16th and 1/32nd note run that spans bars 32-33 of the solo shows how I might use this idea in a soloing context, by ascending the Cadd9 triad into the high register.

Example 1y

Bars 34-35 of the solo show another way that I like to use add9 triads. In bar one we have a ii–V chord change (Dm7 – G7). The ii and V chords make a similar sound because they share important notes in common, and many jazz musicians ignore the ii chord and just play ideas over the V chord. In bar thirty-four (bar one below), I play a Gadd9 triad run over the G7 chord. Gadd9 comprises the notes G, B, D, A and implies a G9 harmony.

This run is repeated, spanning the end of the first bar into the second bar. This time there is no ii–V cadence, it's just played over the C6 chord. This is a superimposition idea. It works to play Gadd9 over C6, because the chords share two notes in common (G and A), and the additional notes that belong to Gadd 9 (D and B) are the 9th and 13th intervals respectively.

Example 1z

Triad Pairs

Bars 17-18 of the solo use the C major and F# major triad pair that we drilled earlier in the chapter. In bar seventeen (bar one below) the third note begins a C major triad, then transitions into an F# major triad. In the first half of bar eighteen (bar two below), you'll hear that we descend the F# major triad, then the C major triad.

Example 1z1

In bar thirty-one of the solo (bar two below) the melodic line begins with a C major triad, transitions into an F# major triad, back into C major, then ends with a Dmadd9 extended triad. (Playing Dmadd9 over an F bass note creates an FMaj7 harmony).

Example 1z2

Borrowed Augmented Triads

Another concept I like to use (which we'll explore further in the augmented triad chapter) is a superimposition idea. Since it's used a few times in the solo, it warrants a quick explanation here.

I mentioned in the introduction that the augmented triad is a close relative of the major triad. That's because they both have major 3rd intervals, and are distinguished only by their 5th. The major triad has a perfect 5th while the augmented triad has a #5.

We can use the augmented triad as a superimposition over a major chord to add tension, and over a dominant 7 chord to add an altered note. Both ideas are used in the solo.

In bar ten of the solo (bar two below), there is a ii–V–I sequence. Here I'm playing a B augmented triad over the whole sequence. The Baug triad works over the G7 chord because it contains two chord tones and adds a #5 or b13 note (D#). Surprisingly, it also creates a nice color over the C major, adding the 7th and a tense sounding #9 (D#, which wants to resolve a half step to E, the 3rd).

Check out this idea some more by jamming over a C major vamp and switching between Baug and C major triads.

Example 1z3

Bar twelve of the solo contains a variation on this idea.

Example 1z4

We can play augmented arpeggios from the root note or 3rd of a dominant 7 chord to create a 7#5 sound. In bar thirteen of the solo, an augmented triad is played over an A7 chord.

Depending on which note in this lick we consider the starting note, we can think of this either as:

- Playing an augmented triad from the root of a dominant chord (i.e., Aaug over A7) or,

- Launching an augmented triad from the 3rd of a dominant chord (C#aug over A7)

Aaug and C#aug contain identical notes, just in a different order, so you can remember this idea whichever way makes more sense to you!

Example 1z5

Here is the same idea used in bar fourteen of the solo (bar one below), where a Baug triad is played over G7 to create a G7#5 sound.

Example 1z6

Now work through the whole solo. I recommend you learn it in sections of a few bars at a time, working on lines that have a clear beginning and end. Also jam out the ideas you've learned in this chapter over the backing track.

Example 1z7 – Full Solo

Em7♭5 B♭7 A7 Dm7 A♭7 G7
C6 C9/E F F♯dim C6/G G7 C6
C6 Em7 A7 Dm7 G7 C6
C6 Dm7 G7 Dm7 G7 C6 Em7♭5 B♭7 A7
Dm7 A♭7 G7 C6 C9/E F F♯dim C6/G G7 C6
T
A
B

C6 Em7 A7 Dm7 G7 C6 C6 Em7 A7
Dm7 G7 C6 Em7♭5 B♭7 A7
Dm7 A♭7 G7 C6 C9/E F F♯dim
C6/G G7 C6 C6 Em7 A7
Dm7 G7 C6 C6 Em7 A7

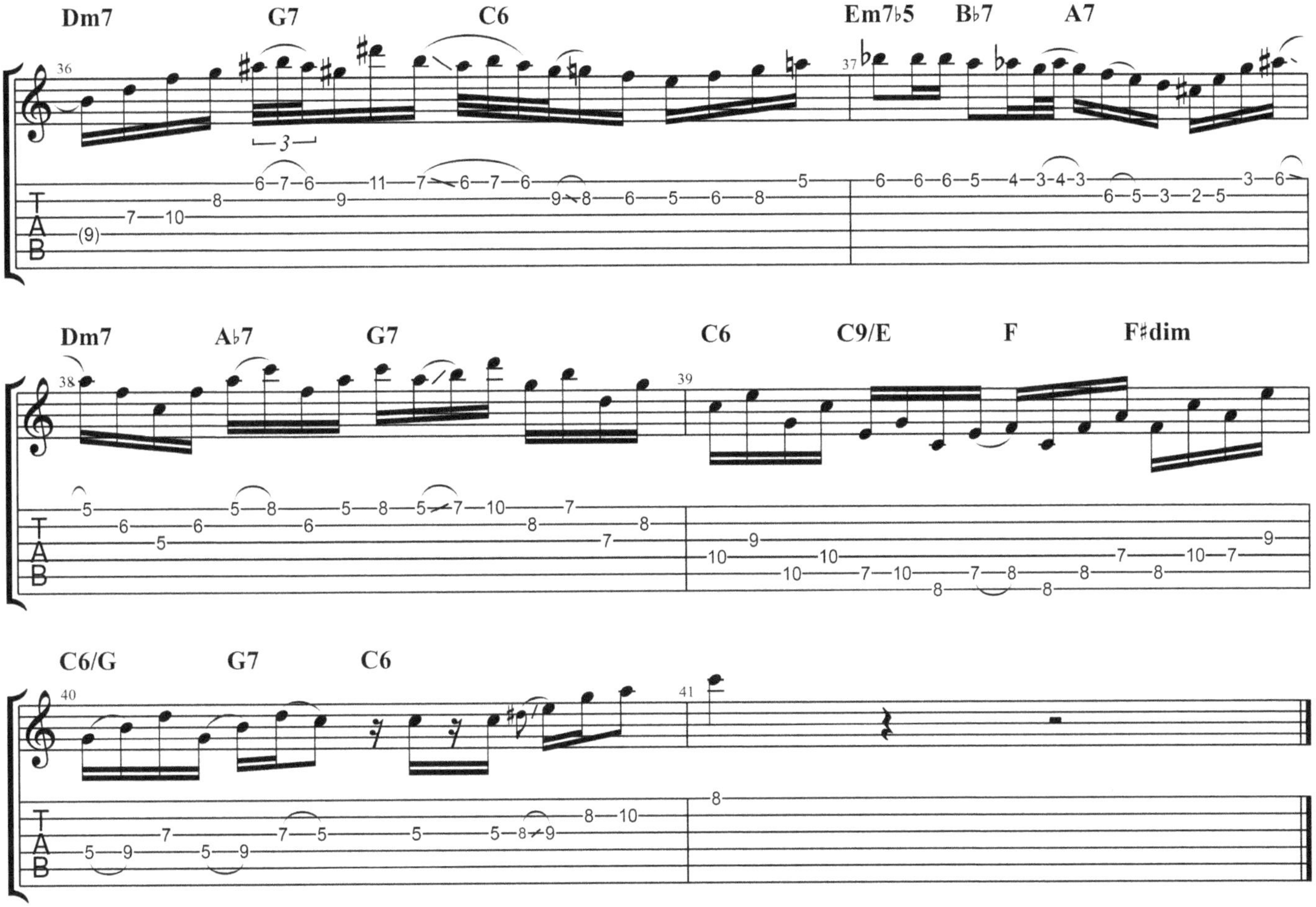
Dm7
G7
C6
Em7♭5
B♭7
A7
Dm7
A♭7
G7
C6
C9/E
F
F♯dim
C6/G
G7
C6

Chapter Two – Minor Triads

In this chapter we're going to look at the second of the four essential triads – the minor triad.

To construct a C minor triad we begin with the C Natural Minor scale (C, D, Eb, F, G, Ab, Bb). Starting on the C note, and stacking 3rd intervals on top, we get C, Eb, G – the root, minor 3rd, and perfect 5th.

To learn this triad we'll follow the same process we worked through in the previous chapter, playing it horizontally across the fretboard, arranged on string sets.

As with the major triad, there are only *three minor triad shapes* on each string set that repeat across the neck.

Also note that the minor triad and major triad only have one note different. The minor triad has a flat 3rd, while the major triad has a major 3rd. The root and 5th remain the same. This is important to know because it means that you can use all the major triad shapes you've spent time learning, and easily transform them into minor triads by lowering the 3rd a half step.

Look at Diagram 1 and you'll recognize the first group of triad shapes you played in Chapter One, just with the 3rd lowered to a b3.

This is one of the keys to memorizing triad shapes.

Of course, you do need to know your intervals to quickly adapt one triad type into another. You need to know where the root is located in each shape, on each string set, so that you know where the other intervals are located in relation to the root. But once you get that down, you'll soon be able to flip between major and minor triads instantly.

Step 1: Visualize the triad across the neck

Here are the three minor triad shapes arranged on strings 6, 5 & 4, beginning with sixth string, root position shape. They are arranged in root position, then 1st inversion (with the b3 as the lowest note), then 2nd inversion (with the 5th as the lowest note)

Diagram 1

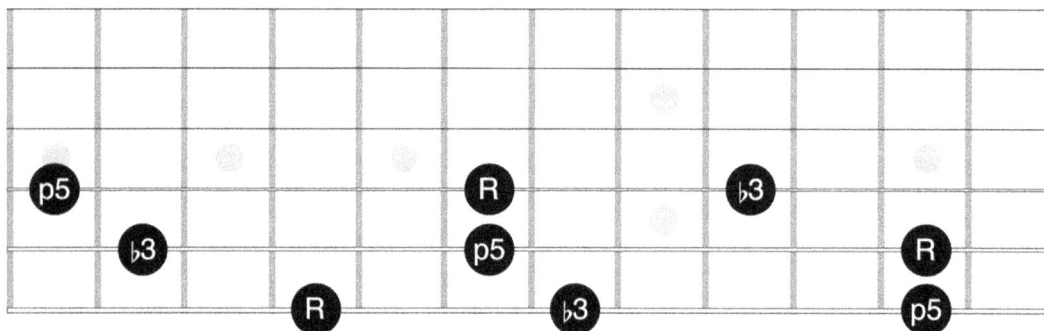

Next, the three minor triad shapes on strings 5, 4 & 3, beginning with the fifth string root note shape, followed by 1st inversion and 2nd inversion shapes.

Diagram 2

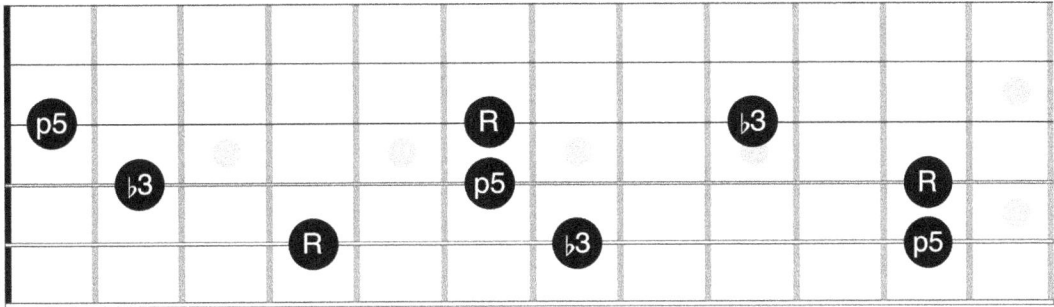

Now we have the three minor triad shapes arranged on strings 4, 3 & 2.

Diagram 3

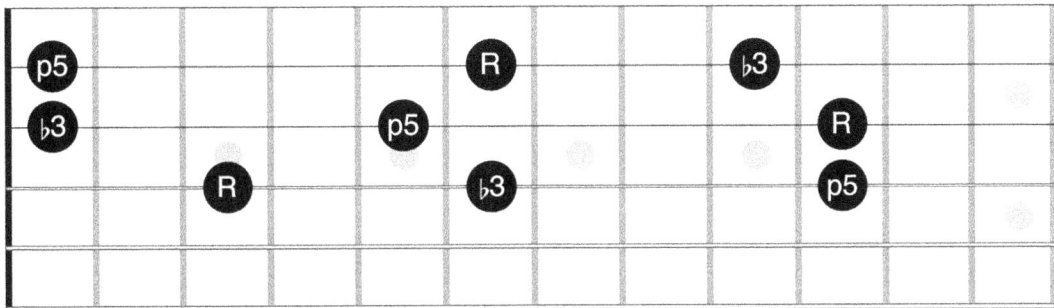

And lastly, the three minor triad shapes on strings 3, 2 & 1.

Diagram 4

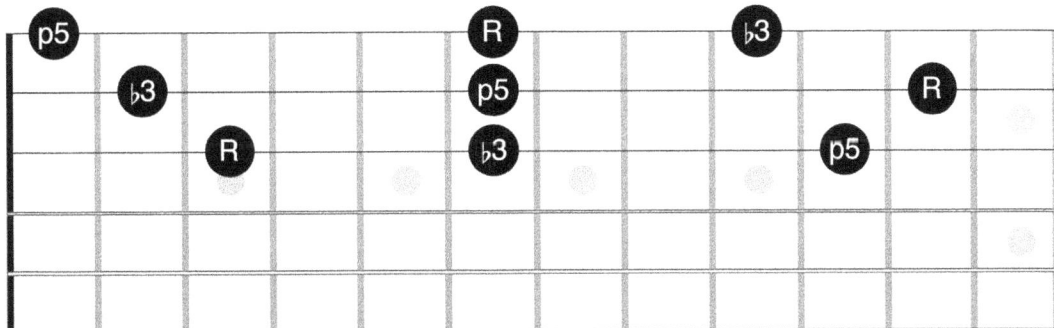

These diagrams have shown you all the locations on the fretboard where you can play *closed voiced* minor triads. Now work through Example 2a, playing the minor triad shapes on each string set, from low to high, horizontally across the neck. Spend some time on this, embedding the shapes into muscle memory.

Example 2a – Closed Voiced Minor Triads

Try to learn the previous exercise by memory, then test yourself on the shapes. Play to a metronome or drum groove and play the shapes in sequence. Next, comp using the shapes and aim to mix them up, moving between shapes on different string sets, and in different zones of the neck.

It's good to learn the minor triad shapes thoroughly on their own to begin with – to make sure you can play them anywhere on the fretboard – but a good exercise to practice is to alternate between major and minor shapes. This will help to reinforce and remind you of the *one-note* difference between the triad types.

This exercise is based on the previous one, but here we alternate between major and minor triads using each shape on every string set.

Example 2b – C Major to C Minor Closed Voiced Triads

Now we'll practice C minor triads across the neck as *open voiced* triads. Like the major triads, these sound more open and are equally useful for comping. Where closed voiced triads are compact and dense, these voicings spell the minor triad sound with more space.

To test yourself, work on some comping patterns that combine open and closed voicings and discover the combinations that appeal to you.

41

Example 2c

Step 2: Essential Triad Patterns

Now we move to Step 2 of the process. Here we begin to drill the minor triad across the neck using pattern-based exercises. This is where we really begin to "hear" the sound of the triad and things become more musical.

We'll apply the same patterns as Chapter One and begin with C minor triads played in a jumping 3rds pattern. As before, play through this sequence nice and slowly. Speed is not a goal at the moment. The initial purpose of this exercise is to memorize the position of the intervals and how they sound. Pick cleanly, with good tone, and work this pattern into your muscle memory.

Don't practice this until you play it perfectly one time. Practice until you can't get it wrong, then work on speeding it up.

Example 2d

Next, the alternative way of playing the jumping 3rds pattern that includes some wider string skips.

Example 2e

Next up, C minor triads played in a contrary motion-type pattern. We begin as before, with the lowest note of each pair ascending then descending a C minor triad from the root, while the top note of each pair ascends then descends the triad in 2nd inversion, and so on.

The string skips and position changes make this a more taxing exercise to nail, so work through it slowly, planning out your fingering and position changes. Remain mindful of the intervals you're playing and the sound they make.

Example 2f

To finish this section, here's an exercise that doesn't follow a specific pattern, we're just playing freeform with the C minor triad all over the fretboard. As previously mentioned, this is a good exercise to test how well you've learned the sound of the triad and its layout across the fretboard. Try inventing your own version of this in your next practice session.

Example 2g

Step 3: Enclosure Patterns

Step 3 means adding approach notes around the C minor triad notes, as we work towards building chromatic enclosure phrases. These are patterns that can create building block phrases you can use to compose melodic ideas. We begin by adding approach notes a half step *below* each triad note, played first around the sixth string root note position, then in 1st and 2nd inversion.

Example 2h

Approach notes placed a half step above the notes of a minor triad sound very dissonant, which limits their usefulness as a melodic phrase, so we're skipping that exercise and moving straight into placing notes a half step below and above C minor triad tones. Taking this approach, the triad notes fall on downbeats and can be clearly heard in the enclosure.

Example 2i

Again, we'll skip the idea of leading with chromatic notes a half step above the triad tones and move into playing C minor triads played as chromatic enclosures. This exercise uses the common bebop approach of:

- Play a note a half step below the triad note

- Play two notes above, descending chromatically

- Play a half step below again

- Play the triad note

The result is a five-note cellular phrase that repeats across the fretboard.

Example 2j

To close out this section, we'll play the minor version of the 1/16th note enclosure lick we learned in the previous chapter. Rather than separating the phrases into five-note cells, we play continuous 1/16th notes with no gaps. We're also extending the pattern here by descending then ascending the idea.

This is a complex line, but try to learn it so that you can play it from memory. It will help to reinforce to triad shapes across the neck, as well as transforming them into a musically useful pattern.

Example 2k

Step 4: Triad Pairs Primer

Now let's explore the sound of minor triad pairs. A common approach in triad pair soloing is to put together two triads of the same quality a whole step apart. This idea works well for the minor triad, so here we will practice playing C minor and D minor triad pairs.

The C minor triad comes from its parent scale of C Natural Minor. However, chord ii in the C Natural Minor scale is not D minor, but D diminished. So, in order to use a D minor triad we need to look to a different scale that contains both chords. In this case, C Melodic Minor fits the bill. In the C Melodic Minor scale, chords i and ii are both minor triads (Cm and Dm).

First, let's listen to the sound they make, alternating between Cm and Dm.

Example 21

You've heard the sound, now let's pause for a moment and consider the effect of superimposing a D minor triad over a C minor harmony. The D minor triad comprises the notes D, F and A. Over C minor, these notes represent the 9th, 11th and 13th (or 6th) respectively.

So, the simple idea of playing the minor triad up a whole step gives us immediate access to the extended tones of a C minor chord, and is a really easy way of adding more color to our lines.

Now let's drill this triad pair with some intervallic patterns.

First, here's a melodic pattern I like to play that treats both triads as four-note cells. We start with the D minor triad played from its 5th interval, then play the C minor triad from its 5th. The first note in each triad is repeated at the end to create the four-note cell.

In bar two, each triad is played from its b3, and in bar three from its root note. From bar four onwards the cycle begins again and ends when we run out of strings.

This is also a great workout to practice your string crossing picking skills.

Example 2m

The next example shows another useful pattern for this minor triad pair. This time we begin with the C minor triad played from its sixth string root. Again the triad is played as a four-note cell by repeating the first note. This position lends itself to smoothly moving into playing the D minor triad played in 1st inversion, and that pattern continues throughout bars 1-3.

In bars 4-6 we play C minor in 1st inversion followed by D minor from its root. The four-note cells change here and the repeated notes are played consecutively, but on different strings and in a different octave. In the final three bars, we keep the new cell pattern, and play C minor from its root and D minor in 2nd inversion.

Example 2n

Step 5: Add9 Triad Sounds

The final step of the learning process is to extend the triad and play some add9 sounds. Remember that we take the C minor triad and add its 9th (D) to form a Cm(add9) (not a Cm9, since there is no b7 present).

First, play up and down the Cm(add9) four-note cell to get familiar with the sound.

Example 20

Let's play the minor add9 triad using the alternate note or "jumping 3rds" pattern we've been using. This example starts from the sixth string root position and ascends/descends. Some of the fingering and position changes are tricky in this pattern. The notation/TAB shows the way I would arrange and play the notes across the fretboard, but if any of it feels too awkward, you can work out an alternative arrangement that feels more comfortable.

In bars 7-9 I also show you a way of playing the triad from its fifth string root in 3rd position, all the way up to the 20th fret. Work out how to play it smoothly descending too! Also investigate different paths you could take to traverse the fretboard.

Example 2p

Next, let's take the ascending "4s" pattern we used for the major triad in Chapter One and apply it to the Cm(add9) triad. If you learned that pattern well, then you might be able to adapt it by flattening every E note to Eb. Otherwise, learn this pattern and most importantly, absorb the sound of the minor add9.

Example 2q

Now play through this sequence, with the Cm(add9) cell played in 1/18th note triplets. Learn it slowly, then gradually work your way up to around 90bpm.

Example 2r

Solo Study

For our minor triad study, we're going to solo over the changes to a classic Bill Withers soul tune. We're going to play it in its original key of A Minor, which means you'll need to think in terms of transposing the minor triad ideas we've explored from C down to A.

We'll also need to navigate the other minor chords in this tune, as the sequence moves between Am, Em and Dm. For reference, here are the notes of each of those triads:

Am = A, C, E

Em = E, G, B

Dm = D, F, A

As in the previous chapter, I'll pick out a couple of bars to highlight where certain triad-based ideas have been used.

Each piece of music is different, and some ideas will better lend themselves to the mood of a particular tune than others. For this piece, I just played what I felt and what I heard in my head. Looking back, I didn't use many triad sequencing ideas, but instead I focused on playing minor triad add 9 phrases, and using minor triad pairs. Let's look at a few examples.

Add9 Triad Phrases

Bars 9-10 open a new chorus of the solo. Let's look at what's happening in bar ten in particular (bar two below). The harmony shows we're playing over Am at this point. The opening phrase is an Am(add9) arpeggio. That's the Am triad (A, C, E) plus the 9th (B).

We also have a superimposition idea here. Over a minor chord, we can play a minor triad located a perfect 5th above i.e., over an Am chord we can play an Em triad. This is quite an inside sound, but the superimposition gives us quick access to the 5th (E), b7 (G) and 9th (B) of Am. The Em triad line begins halfway through bar ten of the solo and continues to the end of the bar.

Example 2s

Bar fifteen (bar one below) begins with a fast Am(add9) phrase. After a bluesy lick over the Em chord, the bar ends by anticipating the Am chord in the bar that follows by playing a four-note Am triad cell.

In bar sixteen (bar two below) I played an Am(add9) line that was further enhanced by adding in the 11th (D). (The G# note here is just a chromatic approach note targeting an A). This five-note arrangement could also be seen as coming from the A Dorian scale.

Example 2t

Triad Pairs

Triad pair sequences are used at various points in the solo. Below, I've pulled out bars 11-12 of the solo to highlight how it's possible to weave triad pairs together in a less obvious way. In the first bar, the melodic ideas are drawn from pairing Am and Bm triads. This gives us a six-note pool of notes consisting of A, C, E (Am) and B, D, F# (Bm). We can handle those notes either by playing the triads as distinct pairs, or we can freely mix up those six notes, treating them as a kind of hybrid scale.

I took the latter approach with this line, attempting to weave together the triad pairs in a less obvious way. It's also a rhythmically challenging line to play, with mixed note groupings, so take your time learning the phrasing.

Example 2u

Here is another complex line that uses triad pairs. We're focusing on bars 17-20 of the solo.

In bar seventeen (bar one below), we open by spelling out the Am(add9) triad. We then begin to blend the Am and Bm triad pairs, ending with a chromatic descent that is targeting a D note at the beginning of the second measure. The second measure is also a blended triad line, with some unusual note groupings.

The third measure opens by playing a Bm triad inversion over the Am chord, which does the job of highlighting its 11th (D), 13th (F#) and 9th (D) intervals. From there we weave in and out of Am and Bm triad notes.

In the fourth measure, we change things up by playing a G major add9 triad over Am. This implies that the Am is chord ii in the key of G Major, and creates a cool A Dorian sound.

Work through this line slowly to nail down the odd note groupings. Listen to the audio example a few times to capture the timing and phrasing.

Example 2v

Now work through the whole solo. Focus on the ideas that jump out to you, aim to memorize them, and make them a part of your vocabulary.

Example 2w –Full Solo

Am
Em
Em/G
Am
Em
Dm
full
full full
Am
Em
Em/G
Am
Am
Em
Em/G
Am
Am
Em
Em/G

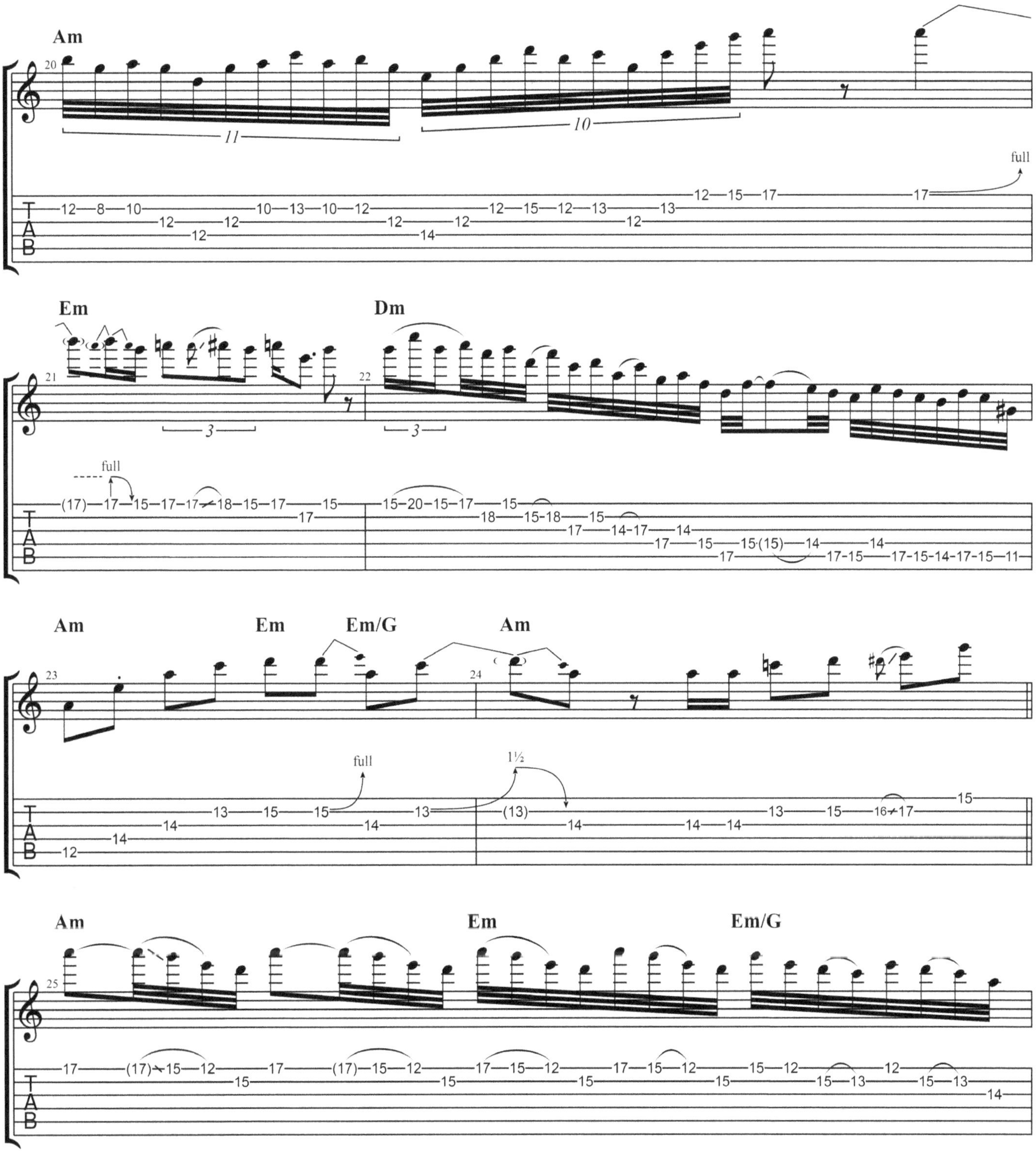
Am
full
Em
Dm
full
Am
Em
Em/G
Am
full
1½
Am
Em
Em/G

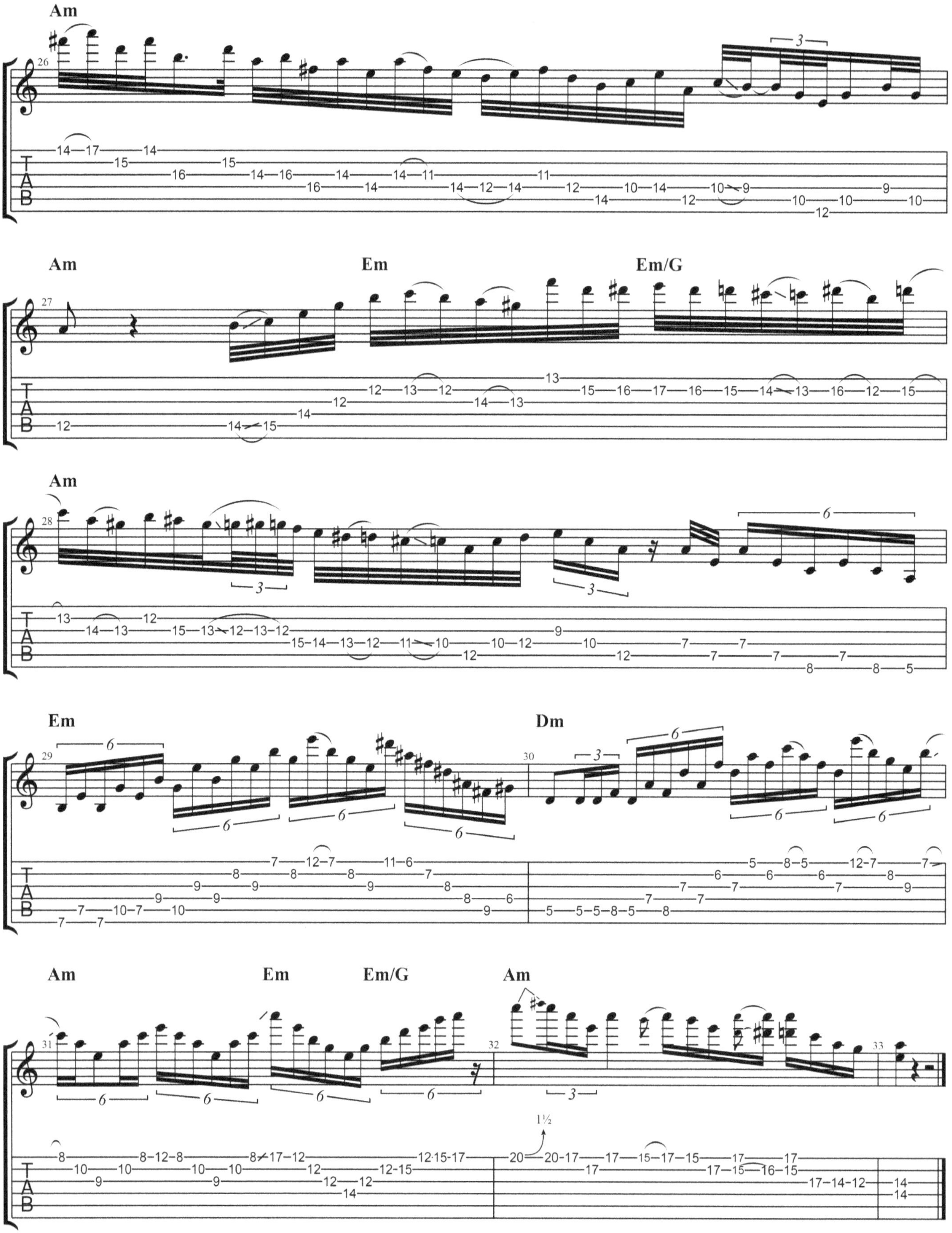
Am
Am
Em
Em/G
Am
Em
Dm
Am
Em
Em/G
Am
1½

Chapter Three – Augmented Triads

In the introduction, I mentioned that the augmented triad can be thought of as a close relative of the major triad. That's because the triads share a major 3rd interval and are differentiated only by their 5th. Where the major triad has a perfect 5th, the augmented triad has a raised 5th.

Compare C major and C augmented triads:

- Major triad formula: 1– 3–5 (C, E, G)

- Augmented triad formula: 1–3–#5 (C, E, G#)

Another way of describing these triads is to say that a major triad consists of a major 3rd interval with a minor 3rd stacked on top, whereas the augmented triad is made up of two stacked major 3rd intervals.

Before we go any further, you may be asking yourself, "I know about the augmented triad, but where can I use it musically?"

The augmented triad naturally occurs in the harmonic and melodic minor scales, as well as the whole tone scale, but that doesn't mean we'll use it only in a minor context. Here are some ways in which we can apply it:

- **Chromatic voice leading**. The #5 interval in the augmented triad wants to resolve, so we can use it to approach other chords chromatically e.g., C augmented leading to A minor, or C augmented to Fmaj7. In the latter scenario, C augmented shares C and E notes with Fmaj7, and its G# note resolves upward to the 3rd (A) of Fmaj7

- **Substitute for an altered dominant chord**. If you look at the shape of a dominant 7#5 chord on the fretboard it's easy to visualize an augmented triad sitting on top. When comping/soloing, we can simplify playing over a C7#5 by using a C augmented triad

- **Superimpose over dominant 7 chords**. First, we can imply an altered dominant sound by playing an augmented triad over a plain dominant 7. But we can also play an augmented triad from the 3rd of a dominant 7 (an idea I used in the study solo in Chapter One) e.g., playing B augmented over G7. There are other substitution possibilities too!

- **Lydian sounds**. Over a C major chord, a C augmented triad hints at the C Lydian Augmented scale (a mode of A Melodic Minor) for a tense outside-inside sound

Step 1: Visualize the triad across the neck

The stacked major 3rd intervals in the augmented triad mean that all the notes are the same distance apart. This fact leads to a series of repeating shapes when we map the triad across the fretboard.

The nature of the augmented triad means that there is only *one shape* per string set, which moves across the neck in major 3rd intervals. The diagrams below show the lowest to highest voicings on the fretboard.

There are only four augmented shapes to learn in order to master it across the fretboard, not the usual twelve! Here is the augmented triad shape arranged on strings 6, 5 & 4. The shape remains the same, and each time we move it, we create an inversion of the triad.

Diagram 1

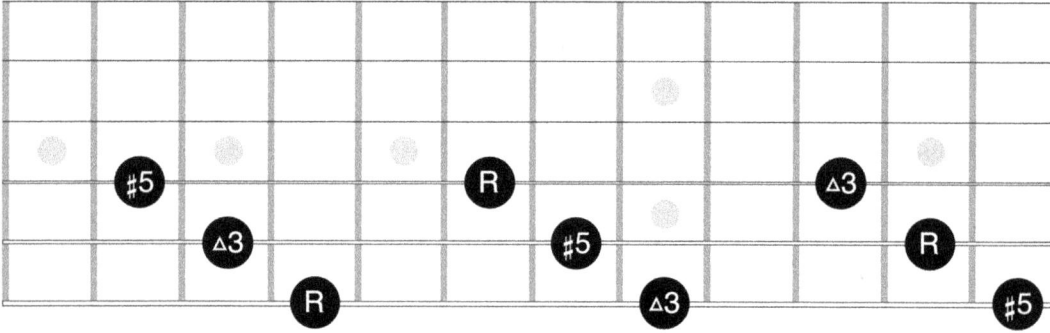

Next, the augmented triad shape on strings 5, 4 & 3.

Diagram 2

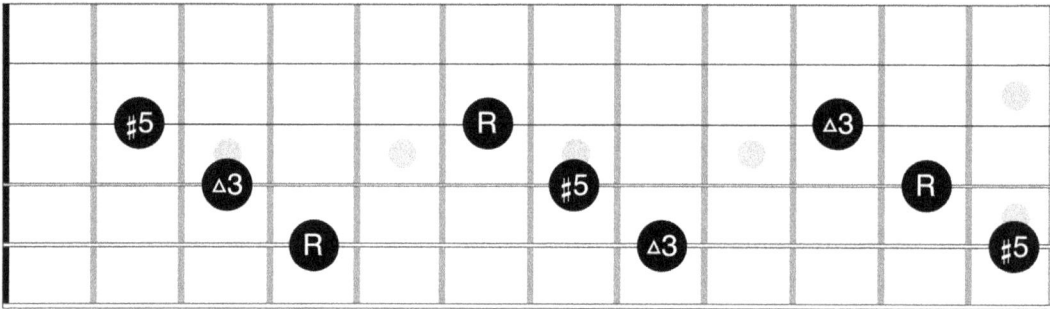

Now we have the augmented triad shape arranged on strings 4, 3 & 2.

Diagram 3

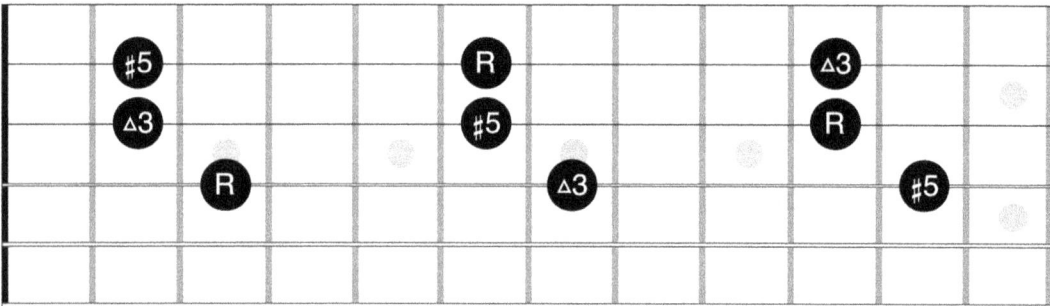

And lastly, the augmented triad shape on strings 3, 2 & 1.

Diagram 4

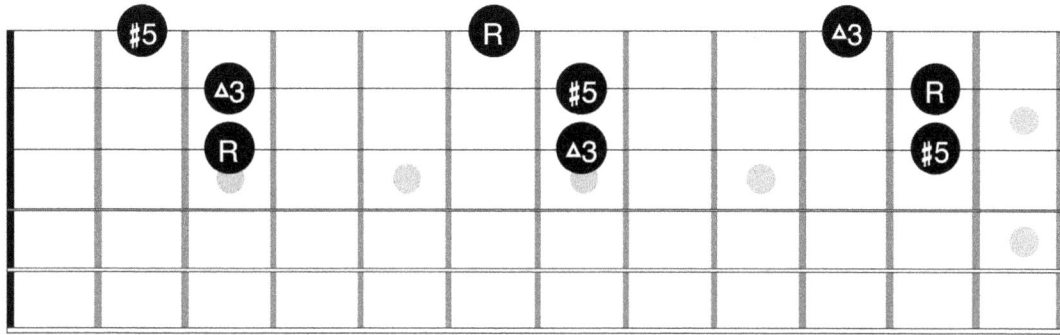

The diagrams have shown all the places on the fretboard where we can play *closed voiced* augmented triads. Now we're going to practice the triad shapes on each string set, from low to high, horizontally across the neck.

Example 3a

Although you'll probably use closed voiced augmented clusters all the time when soloing, if you want to play augmented chords, I prefer these voicings because they sound less dense.

Example 3b

Step 2: Essential Triad Patterns

Next, we'll drill the augmented triad using the familiar sequences we've seen. First, C augmented triads played in the jumping 3rds pattern.

Example 3c

In the "jumping 5ths" pattern we can cover a wider range of the neck. As always, focus on cleanly articulating the pattern and don't worry about playing it fast. Train your muscle memory with the crawling pattern and string skips.

Example 3d

Here's an alternative way to play the previous pattern.

Example 3e

Before we move on, here's an exercise I improvised, playing the augmented triad freely across the neck. After working through it, try to invent your own version of this exercise. I recommend you start by locating the root note everywhere on the fretboard (up the length of each string), then locating the intervals around each root. Over time you'll get better at visualizing the triad on the neck.

Example 3f

Step 3: Enclosure Patterns

Now we move into drilling the augmented triad by building enclosure patterns. First, we'll play the C augmented triad across the fretboard adding an approach note below each triad tone. This creates a very useable melodic pattern that highlights the #5 augmented color.

Example 3g

An enclosure approach that works well with the augmented triad is to combine notes a half step below, and a whole step above each triad tone. This exercise takes the resulting three-note cells and plays them as 1/8th note triplets. You'll notice from the fretboard positioning that we launch this idea from the root, then the 3rd, then the augmented 5th.

Example 3h

♩ = 120

In this drill, we begin by placing an approach note a half step below the target triad tone. Like the previous drill, we want to play a note a whole step above the triad tone, but here we preempt the passing note by adding a chromatic note a half step above it. We also delay playing the triad tone by repeating the note a half step below. The result is a five-note cellular phrase.

Example 3i

Finally, here is the C Augmented triad version of the chromatic enclosure sequence we've played in each chapter.

Example 3j

Step 4: Triad Pairs Primer

Now we'll work through some augmented triad pair drills. With the augmented triad, an approach that works well is to combine two triads a half step apart – in this case, C and B augmented triads. In Example 3k we start with the B augmented triad, ascending from its root. Then we move up a half step and descend the C augmented triad from its #5 to its root.

For the next six-note cell, we make the jump up to the 3rd of the B augmented triad, play it ascending, then move up a half step to descend the C augmented triad. Next, we jump onto the 5th string to repeat the pattern from the #5 of B augmented, and then the pattern starts over.

This is a good picking workout. Whether you favor strict alternate picking, economy picking, or a hybrid approach, it's always a challenge to play shapes that predominantly have one note per string. Make sure you program your muscle memory well at a slower tempo to begin with.

Example 3k

Things start to get a little crazy when we combine C and B augmented triads played in the jumping 3rds pattern. Again, at 120bpm, this is difficult to play cleanly, so work your way up to tempo. It's more important to learn the pattern than play fast.

Example 3l

Lastly, the interval skipping pattern I like to call jumping 5ths, beginning with the B augmented arpeggio moving to C augmented.

Example 3m

Step 5: Add9 Triad Sounds

Now it's time to take the augmented triad into add9 territory and turn it into a four-note cell consisting of C, E, G# plus the 9th (D).

NB: If you're wondering what scale the 9th is coming from, it doesn't actually matter. The 9th interval is the same note as the 2nd, and whether we think of C Melodic Minor, C Harmonic Minor or C Whole Tone, the 2nd is always a D.

First, learn the pattern and more importantly the sound of C augmented add9.

Example 3n

Next, we'll apply the jumping 3rds pattern. If you learned this exercise thoroughly for the major triad in Chapter One, you'll already have the geography of the line under your fingers. This is identical to the major add9 drill, but with the G raised to G#.

Example 3o

Starting and ending in the root position, here is a different path we can take to spell out the Caug(add9) triad.

Example 3p

To make things rhythmically more interesting, here is the jumping 3rds pattern again, this time played with an 1/8th note triplet rhythm. This patterns demands having to cross strings mid-triplet and sometimes play several triplets on one string to keep the pattern going.

Example 3q

Next, let's apply the "ascending 4s" pattern to the augmented add 9 triad. Here, we ascend four notes from the root of the triad, then go back to the second note in the sequence and ascend four notes from there, and so on.

To make the drill more challenging, when we reach the top string we begin to descend immediately without replaying the E note on the first string, 12th fret, so that on the way down the four-note cells fall on different beats of the bar.

Example 3r

Solo Study

To showcase the augmented triad in a live playing situation, this solo is based on the first section of the tune *Juju* by Wayne Shorter, which has an extended vamp on a C7#5 chord. As usual, I'll pick out a couple of bars to highlight where certain triad-based ideas have been used.

First, bar seven is an example of adding an approach note below triad notes to create a melodic pattern. This type of chromaticism works especially well with the augmented sound.

Example 3s

Throughout this solo, you'll hear several places where I played the chromatic phrasing pattern we've used that creates a five-note cell. First, in bars 10-12:

Example 3t

Then also bars 23-24:

Example 3u

Lastly, I'll highlight one example of blended triad pairs. We're pairing C augmented (C, E, G#) and B augmented triads (B, D#, G), but using them as a pool of notes to choose from, rather than playing them as distinct, separate triads. This occurs in a few places, but bars 17-19 are a good example of this approach.

Example 3v

Now work on the complete solo and pull out specific ideas you'd like to add to your vocabulary. This is more important than trying to memorize the whole thing.

Example 3w – Full Solo

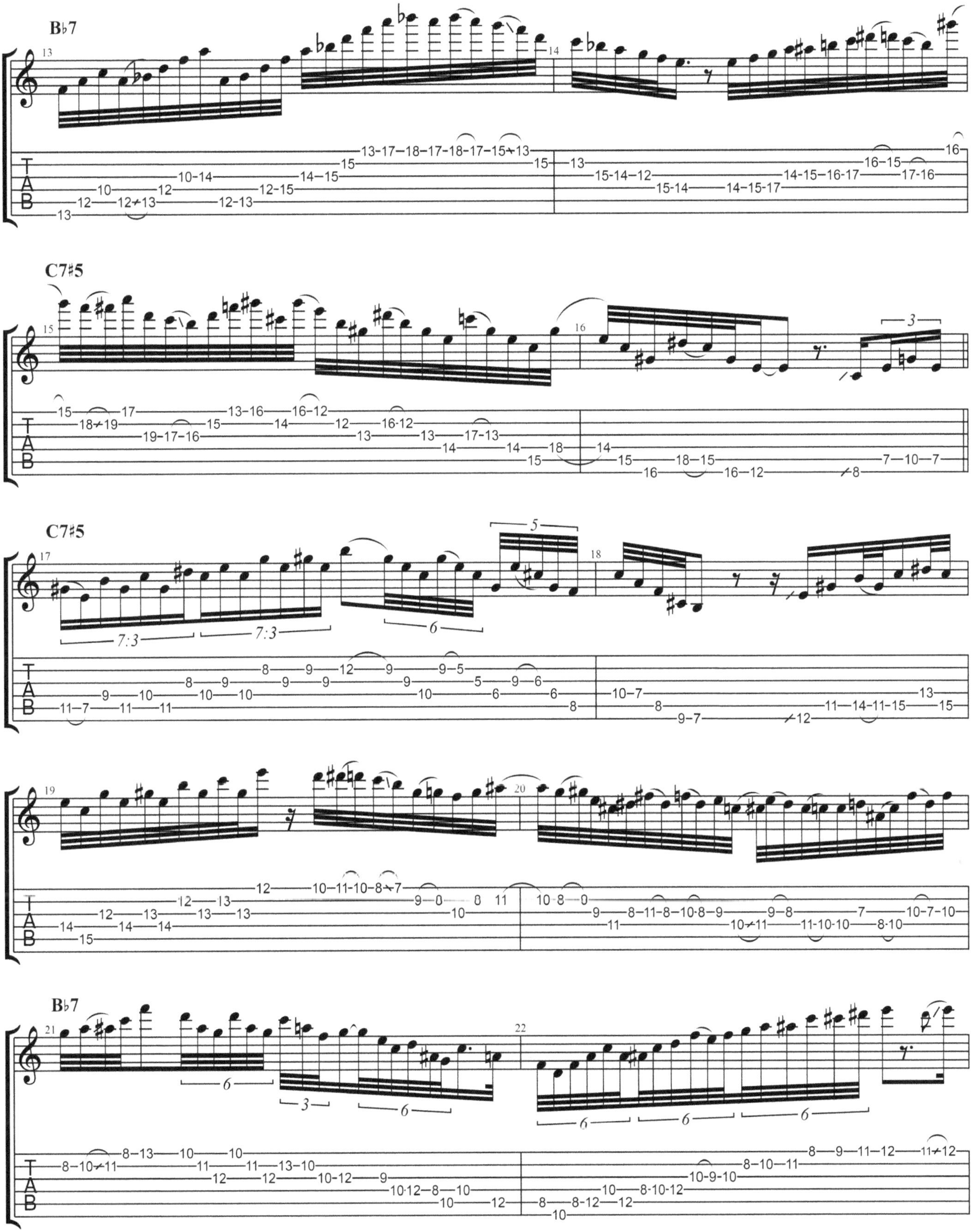
B♭7
C7♯5
C7♯5
B♭7

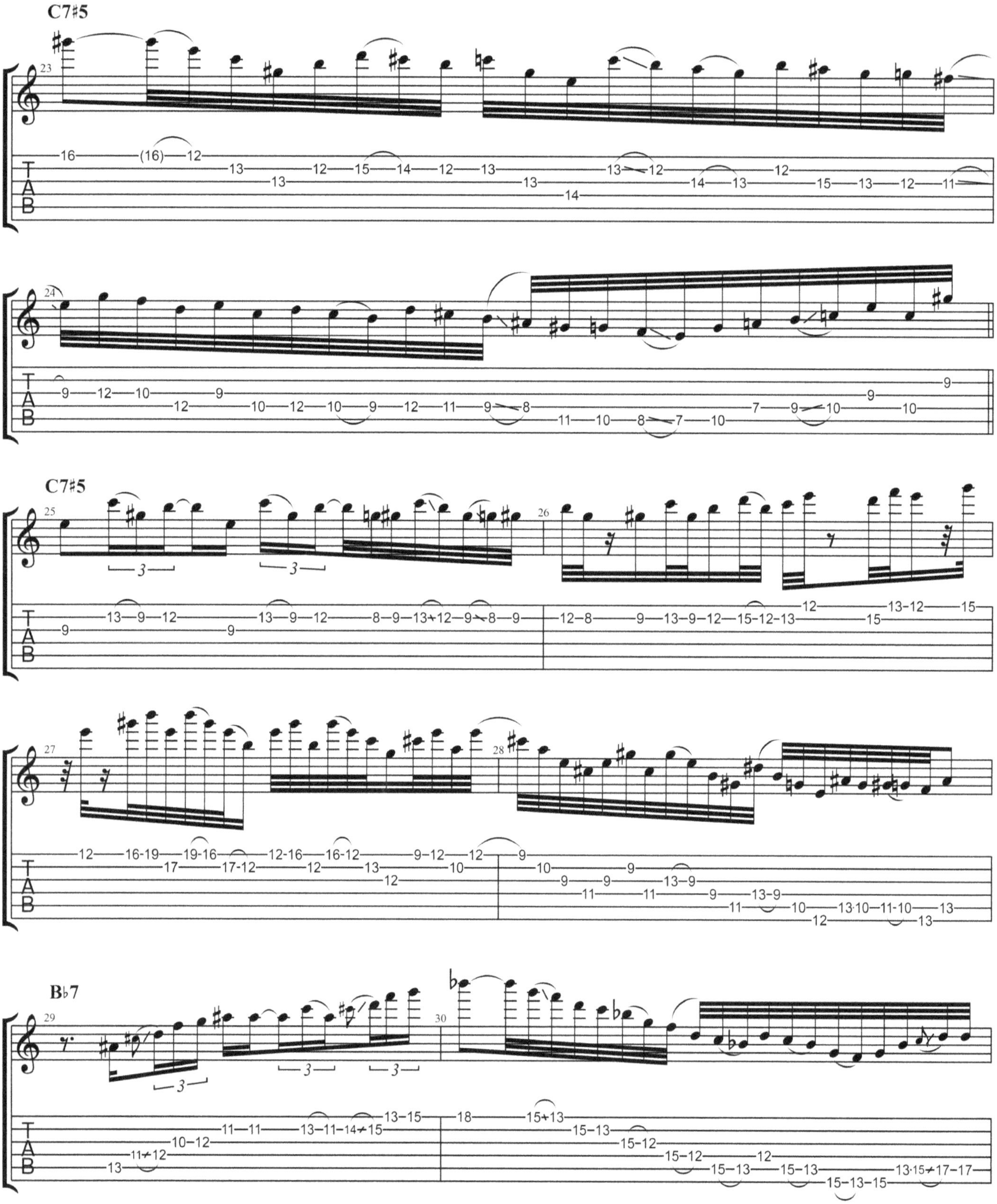
C7♯5
B♭7

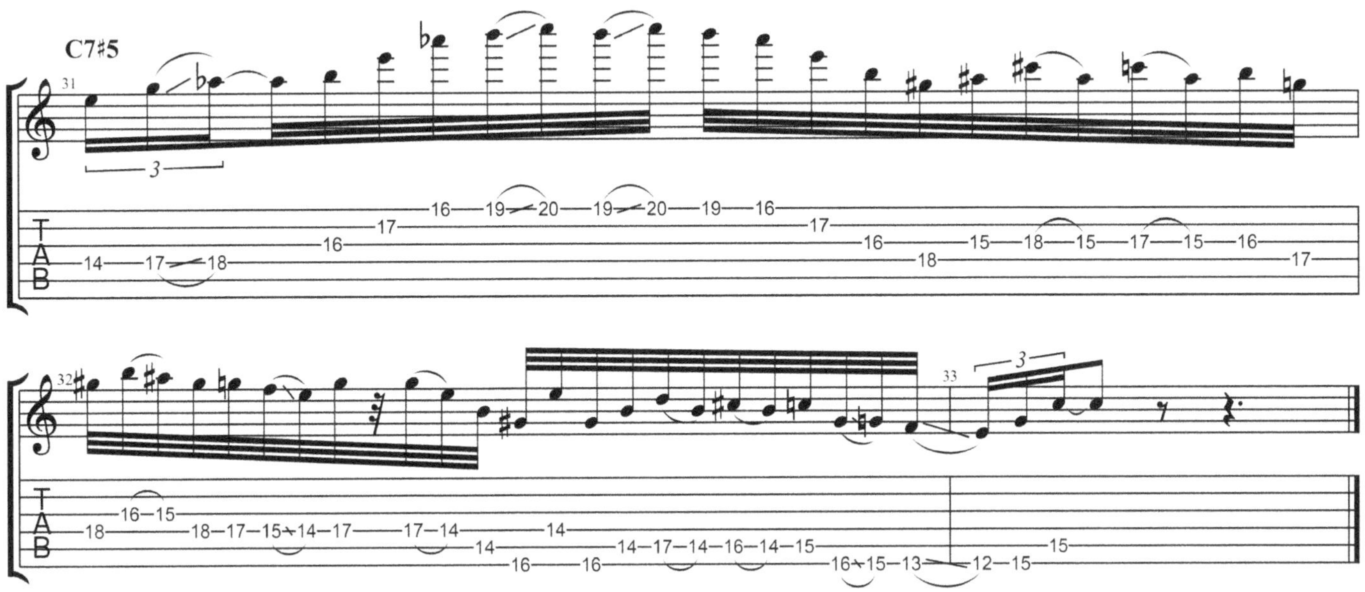
C7♯5

Chapter Four – Diminished Triads

Just as the augmented triad can be thought of as a close relative of the major triad, the diminished triad is a close relative of the minor triad. Diminished and minor triads share minor 3rd intervals and are distinguished by their 5th. Where the minor triad has a perfect 5th, the diminished triad has a flattened 5th.

Compare C minor and C diminished triads:

- Minor triad formula: 1–b3–5 (C, Eb, G)

- Diminished triad formula: 1–b3–b5 (C, Eb, Gb)

Diminished triads naturally occur in major and minor scales (natural, harmonic and melodic) as well as the diminished scale. But how can we use this triad musically?

Diminished triads are the secret sauce of many jazz, fusion and jazz-funk players, as well as modern blues players who want to give their solos a contemporary, outside-inside edge. Here are some ways in which we can apply them:

- **Chromatic connections**. Diminished triads are incredibly useful for connecting other chords. In a chord sequence like Cma7 to Dm7, for example, it's common to add a passing diminished chord (Cmaj7 – C#dim – Dm7). You'll see this idea used all the time in jazz standards. We can play that idea as chords, but we can also imply the connecting diminished chord in our single-line improvisations

- **Substitute for dominant 7b9**. Diminished triads are very useful for quickly creating the sound of an altered dominant chord with a b9. Play a common 10th position G7b9 chord, then take away the G root note and you're left with a Bdim7 chord (B, D, F, Ab). Because of the symmetrical nature of the triad, we can play a diminished triad launching from any of those notes to create a G7b9 sound

- **Using diminished symmetry over vamps**. The repeating nature of the diminished triad makes it a great tool for building movement over a static chord vamp, and allows us to move ideas around the fretboard in minor 3rd intervallic leaps. E.g., cycling through Bdim, Ddim, Fdim and Abdim melodic ideas

- **Outside tension and release**. I don't think of the diminished triad as an "outside" sound really – it's just a more interesting color we can bring into our musical palette at certain moments. But dropping a diminished triad in an unexpected place, then working with it to bring the sound back inside is a really effective way of creating tension and release in your music

- **Hybrid licks**. If we blend diminished triad ideas with major or minor triads, we can create more adventurous, harmonically complex lines that have an in-built chromaticism that sounds intentional

Let's learn the diminished triad across the neck.

Step 1: Visualize the triad across the neck

The interval structure of the diminished triad means that we are back to an arrangement of three shapes per string set. First, here are the diminished triad shapes on strings 6, 5 & 4.

Diagram 1

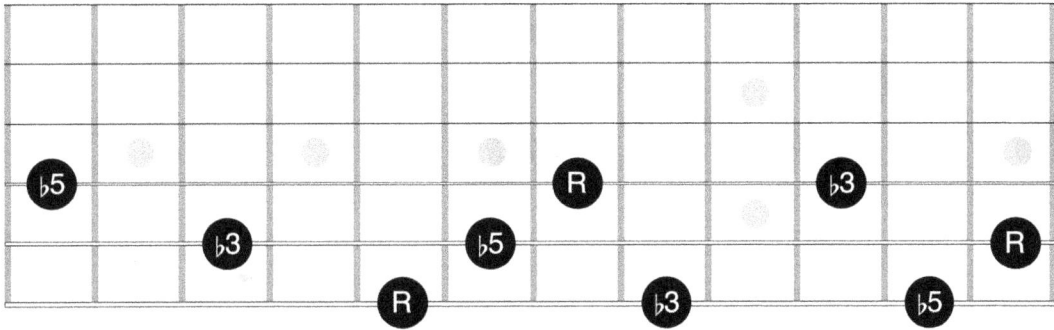

Here are the triad shapes for strings 5, 4 and 3.

Diagram 2

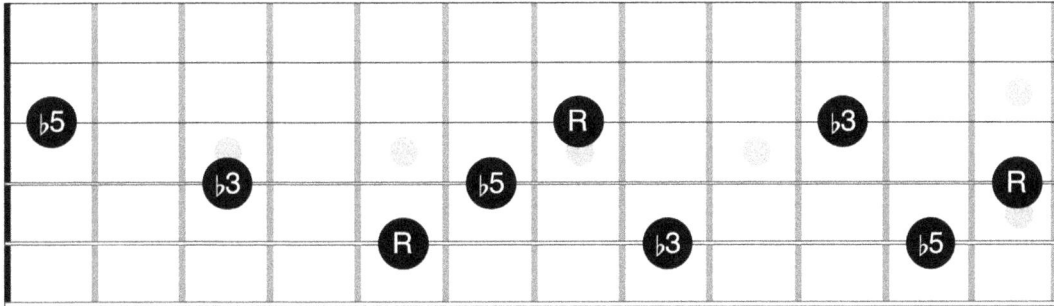

Next, the shapes for strings 4, 3 and 2.

Diagram 3

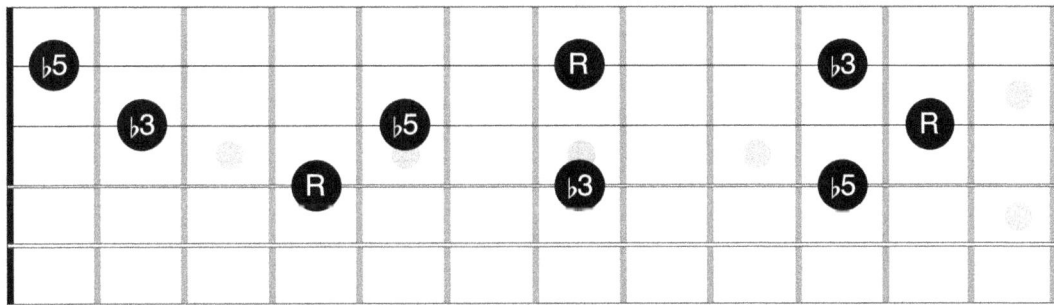

And lastly, the diminished triad shapes on the top three strings.

Diagram 4

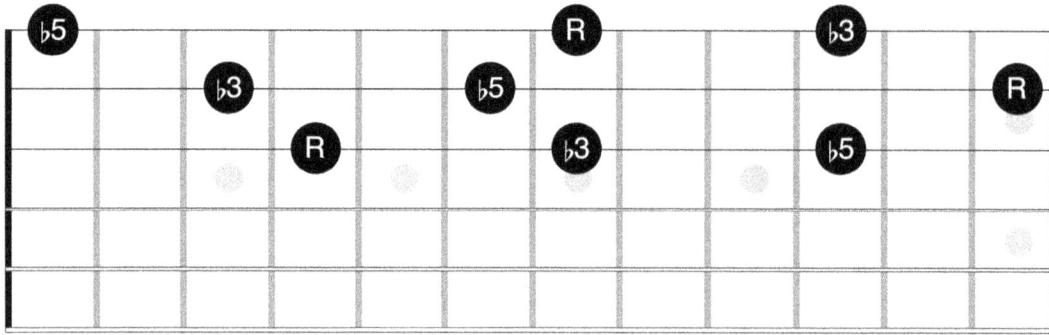

Now we will play C diminished closed voiced triads across the string sets.

Example 4a

Now learn these C diminished open voiced triads across the string sets. You can clearly hear that the diminished triad wants to resolve itself.

Example 4b

Let's move on and drill the diminished triad using the patterns and sequences that should now be very familiar to you.

Step 2: Essential Triad Patterns

Here is the C diminished triad played in the jumping 3rds pattern.

Example 4c

Next, C diminished triads played in the jumping 5ths pattern, which creates more string skips.

Example 4d

You'll have noticed that the intervals of the diminished arpeggio make it awkward to play across the neck. There are some uncomfortable stretches, but it's still a good way to learn the layout of the triad.

Lastly, here is the C diminished triad played freely across the neck. Use a fretboard mapping tool to explore your own pathways across the fretboard.

Example 4e

Step 3: Enclosure Patterns

Now we'll work with some enclosure patterns to further reenforce the location of each triad note across the fretboard. We'll begin as before by playing approach notes a half step below each C diminished triad tone. This naturally conjures up an Eastern-sounding vibe, and could definitely be used as a melodic line on its own.

Example 4f

We can also enclose the diminished triad with notes a half step above and below. The diminished triad always sounds unresolved, but this enclosure sounds pretty tense.

Example 4g

Playing the full chromatic pattern we've been using around the notes of the C diminished triad takes away a bit of the tension, but still leaves us with some exotic inside-out cell patterns.

Example 4h

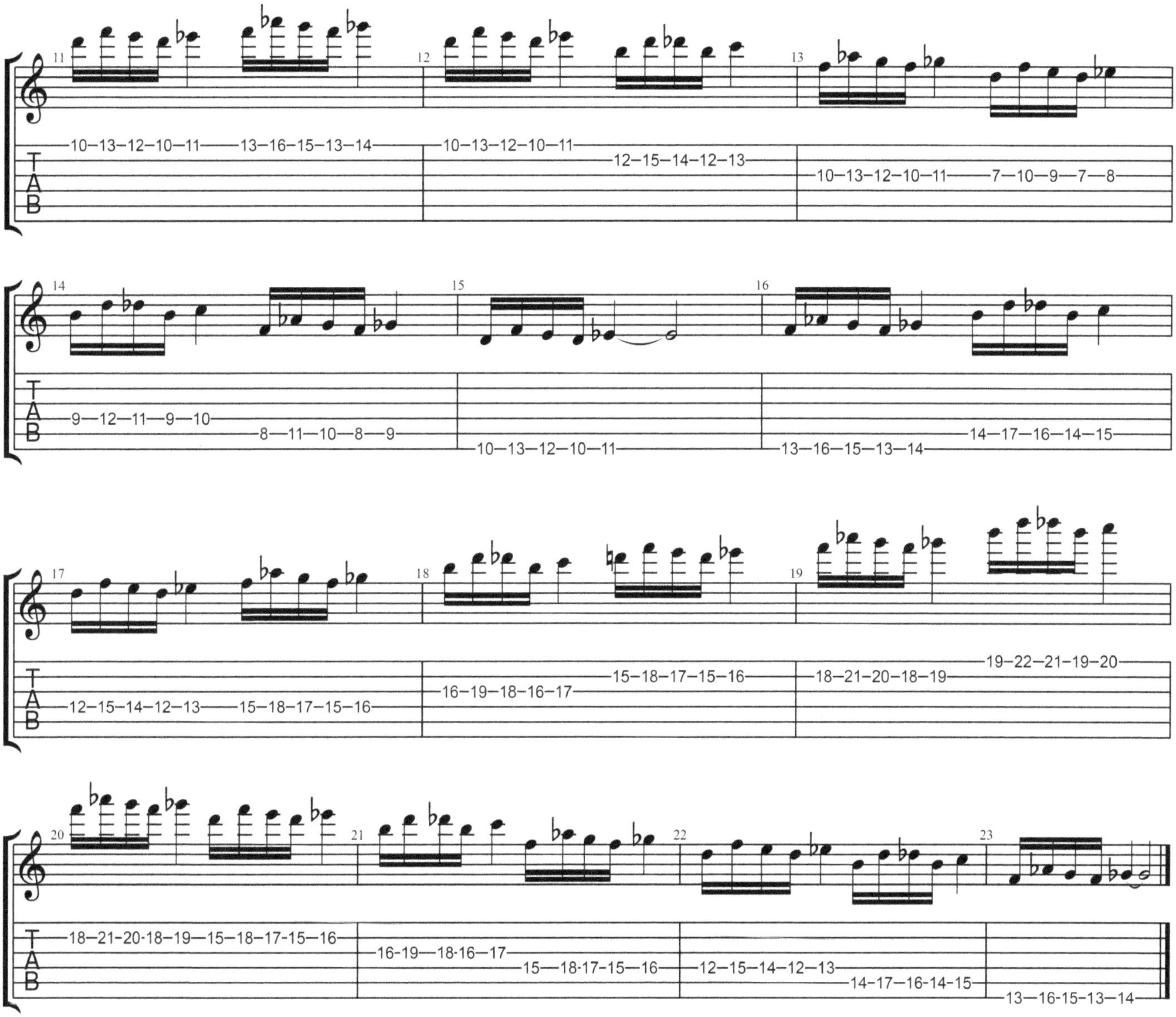

If we turn that idea into an unbroken 1/16th note lick, as we've done in previous chapters, the result is a dramatic lick we can use to traverse the fretboard to target the root note.

Example 4i

Step 4: Triad Pairs Primer

Next, it's time to look at some triad pair drills. Like the augmented triad, the diminished triad lends itself to being paired with a triad a half step away. But whereas with the augmented, we paired a triad a half step *below* the root, with the diminished, we're going a half step *above*, i.e., C and Db diminished. The notes of both triads are:

Cdim = C, Eb, Gb

Dbdim = Db, E, G

This is a good picking workout as you're often required to play one note per string. Make sure you program your muscle memory well at a slower tempo to begin with.

Example 4j

Here is the triad pair played using the descending "3rds" pattern we earlier applied to the minor triad pairs. There are a few awkward movements, so start slow and focus on memorizing the pattern.

Example 4k

This "5ths" pattern is also adapted from the one we used for the minor triad pairs.

Example 41

Next, we move onto C diminished add9 sounds.

Step 5: Add9 Triad Sounds

Here is the C diminished add9 arpeggio pattern (C, D, Eb, Gb) straight up and down. The shape of the add9 triad makes for some tricky fingering and position changes, so work that out beforehand, then try to memorize the shape of it across the fretboard. Don't be discouraged if it takes quite a while to achieve faster tempos – it's more important to learn the shape and play it cleanly. Remember that this is the same pattern as the minor add9 triad, but with a flattened 5th interval (G becomes Gb).

Example 4m

♩ = 120

Next we have Cdim(add9) played in the jumping 3rds pattern.

Example 4n

♩ = 120

Cdim(add9)

Now let's play the add9 triad in jumping 3rds but with an 1/8th note triplet rhythm.

Example 4o

And now in the ascending/descending "4s" sequence.

Example 4p

Now it's time to move on to look at the solo study.

Solo Study

This solo study is based on my arrangement (or *derrangement* as I like to call it) of the Thelonious Monk tune *Bemsha Swing*, which you can hear on my album *Triple Play*. I reduced the changes of that tune down to just two chords and turned it into a modal vamp. The result is an eight-bar structure moving between C7 and F7. I often like to play over very simple chord structures like this, because it gives me more freedom to highlight whatever extended colors or tension notes I like in my melodic lines.

Throughout this solo I'm working with the Cdim and Dbdim triad pair we've practiced – though not always in an obvious way. There is limited mileage to be had from playing one triad after the next in an alternating pattern. There are only so many ways we can do that before it starts to sound predictable!

Instead, I try to fuse the notes of the triads together to create a six-note hybrid scale. In this solo, occasionally I went a step further and combined the notes of Cdim7 and Dbdim7 arpeggios, resulting in an eight-note pattern. Let's look at those two chords:

Cdim7 = C, Eb, Gb, A

Dbdim7 = Db, E, G, Bb

Another way of looking at this collection of notes is to say that the combined diminished 7 chords create the C Half-Whole Diminished scale – a symmetrical octatonic scale.

While this is true in theory, in practice I'm still focused on building melodic lines out of the two basic diminished triads, then expanding them by adding notes around them. If you keep simple triads as your framework for soloing, your lines will always have a solid grounding.

Dominant chords are the ideal scenario in which to play ideas using diminished triads.

C7 contains the notes C, E, G, Bb – root, 3rd, 5th and b7.

The Cdim triad contains the root (C), b5 (Gb) and #9 (A) notes of the chord.

The Dbdim triad contains the 3rd (E), 5th (G), b7 (Bb) and b9 (Db).

So, the triad pair covers all the notes of C7, then adds the possibility of b5, b9 and #9 tension notes, to suggest different altered dominant sounds.

Now let's look at a couple of examples from the solo. In these examples I want to highlight some advanced triad soling concepts you can experiment with over the coming months.

Playing the diminished triad from the b9 of the I chord

At the opening of the solo (beginning with the last note of bar two, going into bar three) we play a Dbdim7 arpeggio over the C7 chord.

When soloing with diminished triad pairs you don't always have to begin with the triad played from the root note – you can jump straight in with its pair i.e., the triad played from the b9 (Db in this case).

Play through this line and you'll also see that I play approach notes a half step below the Dbdim7 chord tones. The phrase at the end of bar three into bar four descends from the Dbdim triad back into the Cdim triad.

Example 4q

Playing triad pairs from the 3rd of the dominant 7

An idea used extensively in Gypsy Jazz is to play a diminished arpeggio from the 3rd of a dominant 7, i.e., over a C7 chord we would play Edim. We can take this a step further, however, and use an Edim and Fdim triad pair over C7 to extend the tension notes. This idea is seen in bar twelve of the solo, where we flip between Edim and Fdim triads. This is also a nice sequencing idea to move between the triads.

Example 4r

Blending I and IV chord diminished triads

In bars 5-7 of the solo, the progression is two bars of F7 moving into C7. For the F7, we could take the same approach as we did for the C7 and play diminished triads from the root and b9, i.e., over F7 play Fdim and Edim triad pairs.

Alternatively, we can blend the triads from the root notes of the IV and I chords, i.e., Fdim moving to Cdim – both played over an F7 chord.

This idea makes sense because C7 is the tonal center of this piece, and the F7 is functioning as the IV chord, which wants to resolve back to the I.

In this line, I begin by playing Fdim to highlight the F7 chord, then descended a Cdim triad. You'll see that I switch back and forth between the triads throughout the line.

Example 4s

This final example is taken from bars 14-16 of the solo. In bar one, over F7, the melodic line comes from blended Cdim and Fdim triads. For the C7 bars, we take the more standard triad pair approach. The triads being used are indicated above the notation in this example, so you can get a feel for how and when we are switching between them.

Example 4t

Now, here is the solo in full to work through. Again, it would be a bit mind boggling to learn the whole thing, so focus on extracting melodic patterns that appeal to you, and work on adding them to your vocabulary. Aim to have something amazing to play over a dominant 7 chord!

Example 4u

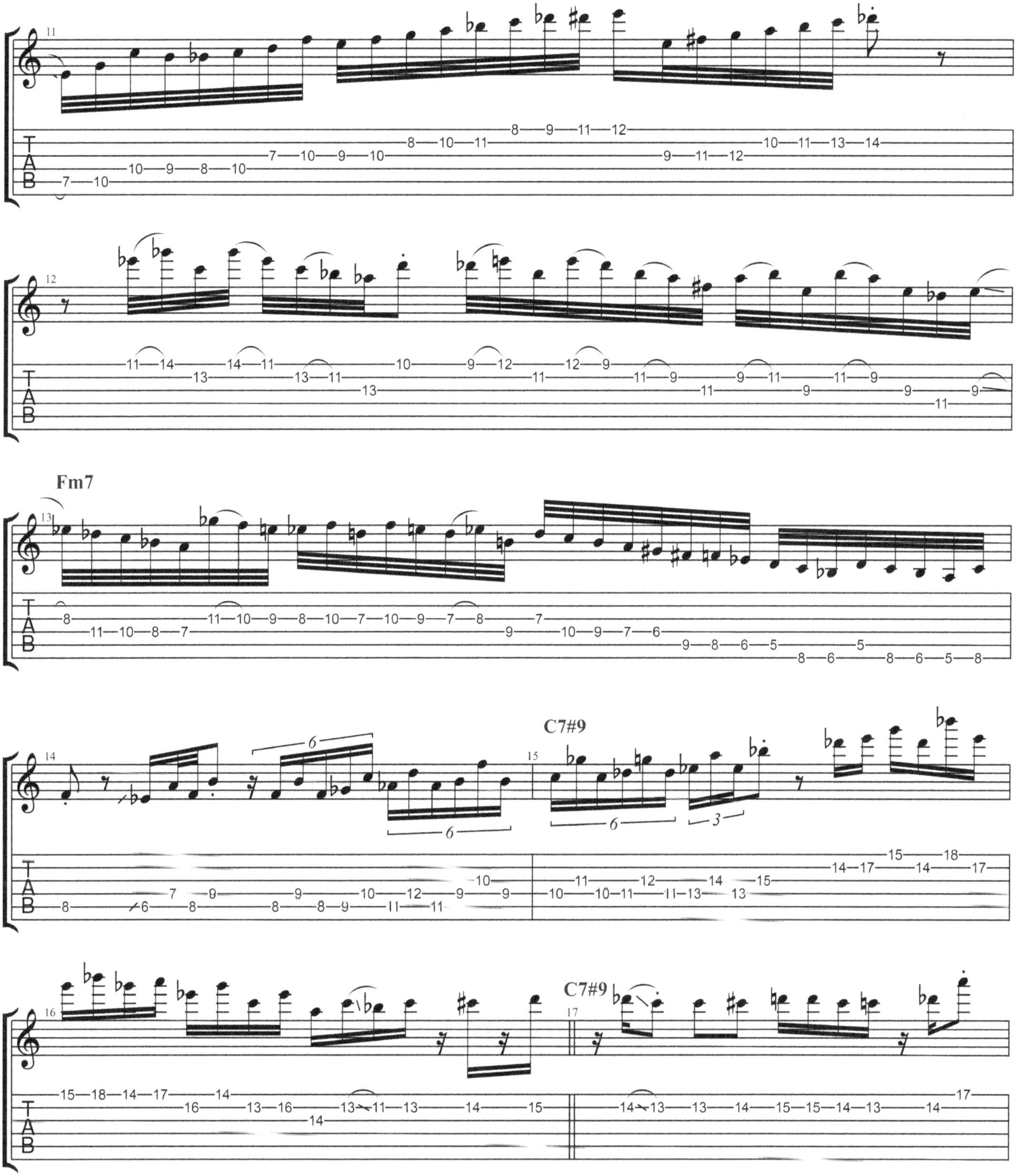
Fm7
C7#9
C7#9

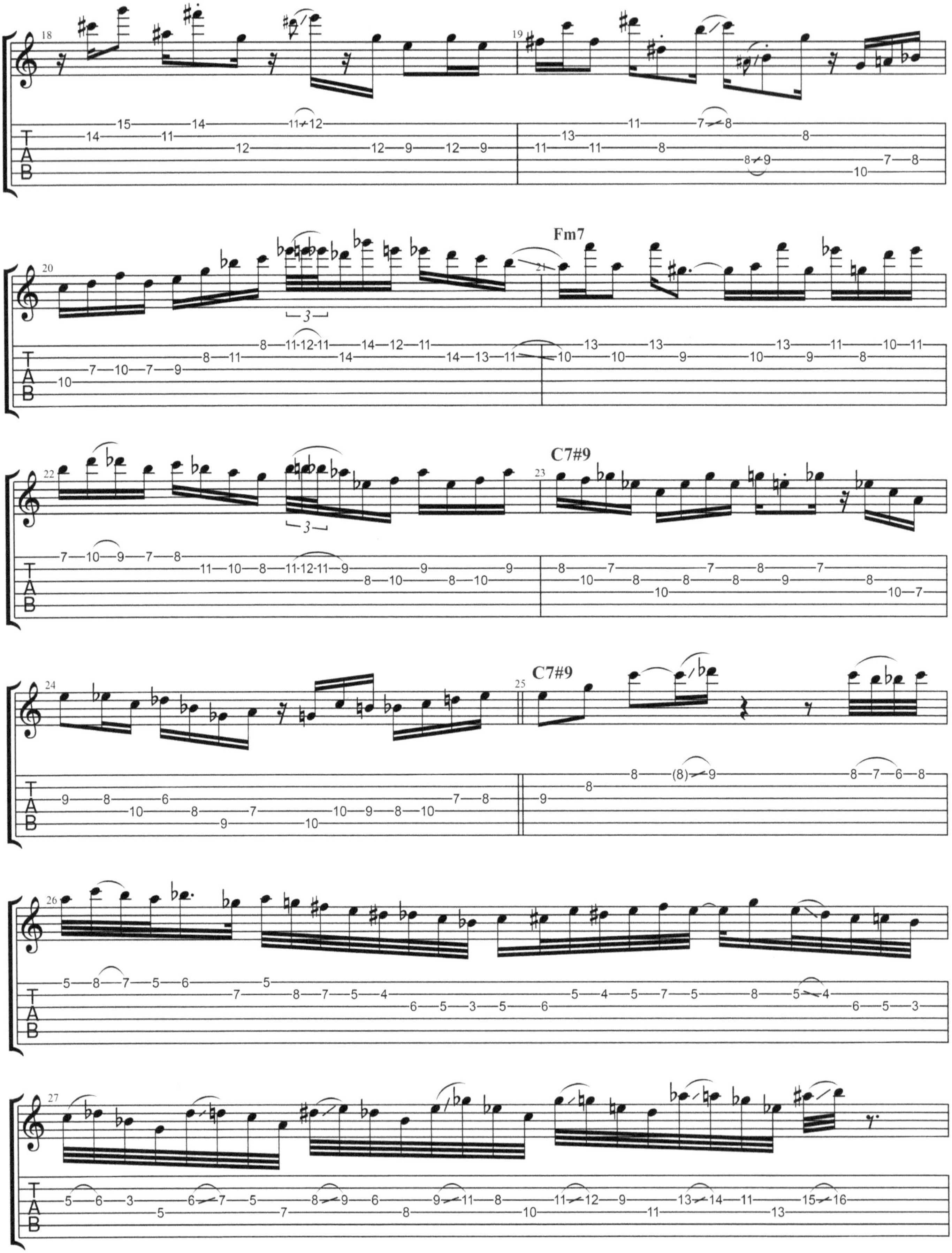
Fm7
C7#9
C7#9

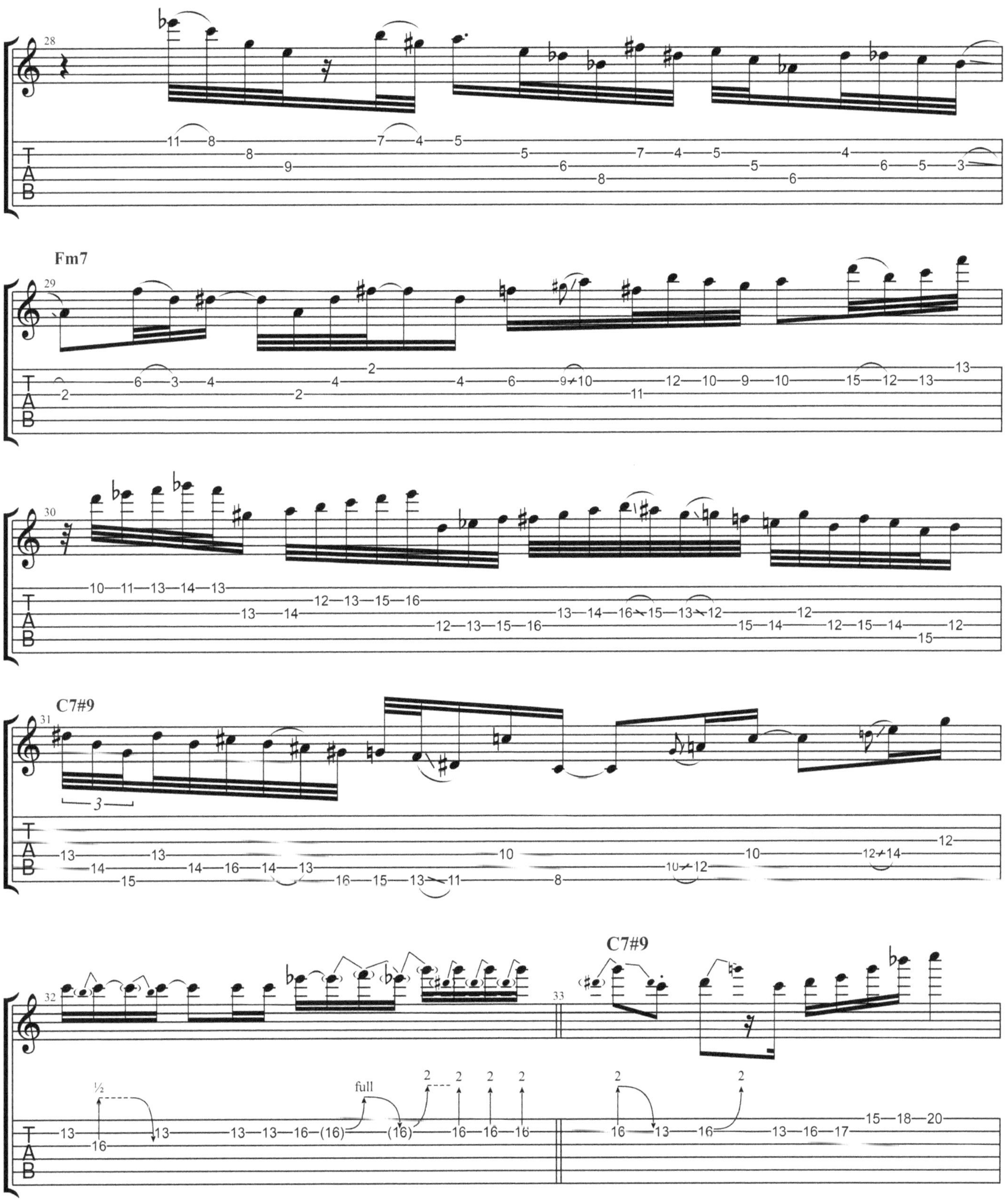
Fm7
C7#9
full
C7#9

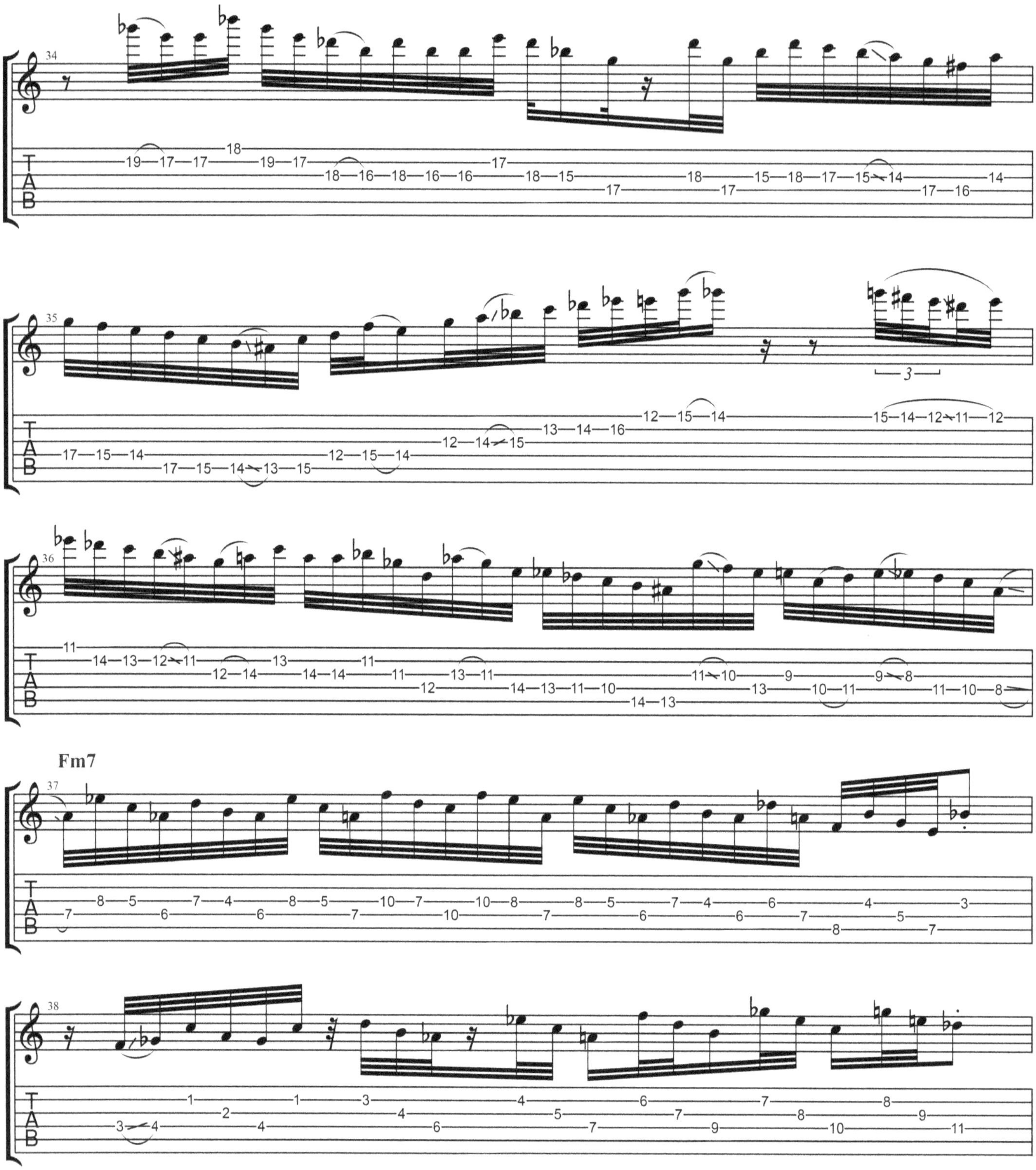
Fm7

C7#9

Conclusion & Practice Plan

Over the course of this book we've tackled the four triads that are the most important to master. If you keep working with these triads, using the drills and melodic ideas in this book, you'll eventually know them inside out, and that will give you an incredible foundation and arsenal of ideas to play any kind of music. You'll be equipped to play chords – and develop melodic lines out of those chords – all over the fretboard, and I guarantee that the ideas you play will be more grounded and more exciting.

We worked with the major triad – the foundational building block of all harmony – and made it more sophisticated by using its add9 triad form and triad pairs. Next, we drilled the minor triad and discovered how to easily add extended color tones by combining minor triads a whole step apart.

The augmented triad we looked at next has its own ambiguous sound and a symmetrical pattern across the fretboard. Superimposed over dominant 7 chords, it gave us access to some outside-inside tensions while retaining a strong sense of melody.

Finally, the dark diminished cousin of the minor triad gave us the tensest sound of all, and we discovered how diminished triad pairs can cover nearly all of the altered tensions it's possible to add to a dominant 7 chord, making it ideal for modern blues or dominant chord modal soloing.

I'll leave you with this suggested practice plan for focusing on a specific triad:

Week 1-2: Visualization working with voicings

- Play closed and open voiced triads across all string sets

- Practice switching between root, 1st, and 2nd inversions

- Play triads horizontally across the neck and work on changing keys (pick a favorite chord progression to practice with)

Week 3-4: Essential Patterns

- Drill triads using jumping 3rds and contrary motion (5ths) patterns.

- Practice triads in freeform to explore the fretboard.

- Apply patterns to backing tracks or vamps and practice using them melodically as part of an improvised solo

Week 5: Chromatic Enclosures

- Practice adding half-step enclosures below, above, and around triad tones

- Practice creating five-note enclosure cells and connect them across positions

- Play enclosure-based licks in time with a metronome

Week 6: Triad Pairs

- Choose a triad pair (e.g., C minor and D minor) and practice alternating them in various rhythmic patterns

- Use both diatonic and non-diatonic triad pairs to explore inside and outside sounds

- Compose one or two licks using triad pairs

Week 7: Add9 Triads

- Practice add9 arpeggios in root position and across the fretboard.

- Work on incorporating add9 patterns (e.g., jumping 3rds, "4s" sequences, triplets) into a solo

- Record yourself playing add9 triad licks over a static vamp

Ongoing

- Work through a solo study in the book, focusing on 2–4 bars at a time

- Work on transposing triad-based licks to new keys

- Integrate triad ideas with scales, bends, slides, and rhythmic phrasing to develop your own personal voice

Good luck and, above all, have fun with it!

Oz